Green Shingles

Green Shingles

At the Edge of Chesapeake Bay

PETER SVENSON

Faber and Faber, Inc.
A division of Farrar, Straus & Giroux
NEW YORK

Faber and Faber, Inc.
A division of Farrar, Straus and Giroux
19 Union Square West, New York 10003

Library of Congress Cataloging-in-Publication Data

Svenson, Peter.
    Green shingles : at the edge of Chesapeake Bay /
Peter Svenson. — 1st ed.
        p.   cm.
    ISBN 0-571-19961-5 (alk. paper)
    1. Chesapeake Bay (Md. and Va.)—Description and travel.
2. Chesapeake Bay (Md. and Va.)—History.   3. Chesapeake Bay
(Md. and Va.)—Environmental conditions   4. Chesapeake Bay
(Md. and Va.)—Social life and customs.   5. Svenson, Peter.
    I. Title.
F187.C5S94   1999
975.5′18—dc21   98-42462

Material adapted from *Green Shingles: At the Edge of Chesapeake
Bay* was previously published in *The Washington Post Magazine*
and *Chesapeake Bay Magazine*

For Van, Allyson, Hope, and Matt

I would like to thank the one who shares my life for her gentle encouragement and sharp editorial eye.

I also offer my thanks to Dolly and Sam McSorley, Donald Schwab, Bill Palmer, J.P. Stephenson Dann, Donald E. Jaccard, William K. Betts, Dan Weaver, and Hope Steele.

Green Shingles

Introduction

We, K and I, united at an age when remarriage begins to look like a tired game of nuptial chairs, know we have it in us to make an attempt once more, this time together, at castle-building.

We are situated in Greenbelt, Maryland, a 1930s-era outlying experiment in social engineering, loops of rowhouses on a web of streets and footpaths, now hard against the nonstop thunder of the Capital Beltway. Our modus vivendi is to get away on weekends when the weather is nice. We hike along the C&O Canal towpath and picnic on either the Maryland or the Virginia side of the Potomac's Great Falls. We visit Harper's Ferry, Manassas, Antietam, and Gettysburg. We descend upon historic inns and choose entrees from calligraphic dinner menus followed by sinful dessert trays. But we look forward the most to crossing the Chesapeake Bay Bridge and entering a region that has everything we wish we lived with on a daily basis: the land-water-sky trinity of Maryland's Eastern Shore.

To the casual visitor from the Washington-Baltimore metropolitan area, the Eastern Shore is near, yet separate from, everything that pertains to . . . Washington and Baltimore. Its farms and flatlands interspersed with tenacious small towns exude a distinctive charm, but the overall proximity to water is what tilts the visitor's predisposition. Magazines and books aplenty sing the Eastern Shore's praises, and no major east-coast newspaper goes too long without an article pertaining to some aspect of its touristic lure. The magic of crossing five miles of bay, with its myriad tints and moods, is reason alone to make the trip.

At first, our visits consist of driving over the bridge, noodling around for a few hours, and leaving with the waning light. Once or twice we stay overnight and go mushy with thoughts of what it would be like to live there. As our trips add up, we start to realize how lightly we're scratching the surface; we're flitting from sight to sight, town to town, skimming the shallowest knowledge and lore. Like any other pair (or carload) of temporary bridge-crossers, we are not without ties to culture, career, and family on the western side of the bay. This is a trek into the boondocks for us, yet we note how increasingly reluctant we are to turn around and go back.

chapter
1

Something beyond mere girder and cable lifts our spirits whenever we cross the water. Riding snugly at sixty miles per hour, our eyes graze the strip-feast of commerciality—outlet centers, fast-food joints, gas stations, real estate offices, boat sales—pervading these first few miles of terra firma, the breadth of Kent Island, before a second bridge, a six-lane hump of concrete, conveys us deeper into Queen Anne's County. Although here is additional corporate allure, the natural landscape seems to be opening up. We're sensing the luxury of elbow room and the foreknowledge that beyond the pavement lies water. The sight of yachts and wharves, of aluminum masts delineating marinas, of parking lots with boat trailers, reinforces our conviction that others feel the same way about it that we do. The billboards and build-up read as a collective invitation: *welcome to another way of life*. In the words of Captain John Smith, Chesapeake Bay's earliest Anglo-Saxon discoverer and pitch-man, "Heaven and earth never agreed better to frame a place for man's habitation."

Bisecting the updated version of Smith's estuarine wilderness, the multiple lanes of U.S. 50 ribbon eastward, conveying daily, in season, tens of thousands of motorists to the Atlantic resorts. We don't travel that far: we poke around Queen Anne's, Kent, and Cecil Counties, looking for nothing in particular—just looking—but almost without knowing it, we've crossed that mental Rubicon to actively seeking. And what are we seeking? Why, a place to habitate, of course! There's no determining moment; repeated exposure infects us. We peel off from the Route 50 slipstream at the northward fork of Route 301, turning northwest onto two-lane Route 213. Our destinations become the realty offices in Centreville, Chestertown, and Cecilton. We have a notion of staying within a forty-five-minute radius of the Bay Bridge, so as not to stray too far from everything that connects us to the other side of the water, but we're definitely ready to contemplate a move.

At this point, we're in the market for that elusive property that fulfills our pie-in-the-sky requirements of affordability, privacy, spaciousness, ease of maintenance—and water frontage, if at all possible. We must fit a growing profile: a remarried two-income couple with cash from a home sale. The first thing realtors ask is how much we're prepared to spend, because the word *waterfront* means adding a hundred thousand dollars right off the bat to the price tag. Everybody wants waterfront, period. Exchanging worried glances, we swallow hard. It means we'll have to borrow more money—so what else is new?

Then, the realtors want to know if we plan to build a home or buy a pre-existing one. Building from scratch is an option many waterfront first-timers choose when they've got capital gains in the bank and they truly want to start over. This dovetails nicely with the offerings of tract developers in cahoots with realtors, some of whom are one and the same person. Charming "coves," formerly farm fields now sliced into long and narrow lots that satisfy a county zoning board and give each property a sliver of creek, abound along the miles and miles of shoreline. Although I'm not too keen on constructing a house again (I've already built four), we don't rule it out.

The next thing the realtors inquire about is the depth of our boat's keel. Waterfront property listings always include the mean water depth as a service to boaters. All we own—and will own for some time to come, judging by the price of a prospective place to put it—is a sailing canoe with a keel no deeper than three-quarters of an inch. This admission on our part invariably draws guffaws.

Further qualifiers ascertained from us as we sit across from realtors' desks have to do with our flexibility insofar as attaching ourselves to one particular locale or community. Nah, we don't have our hearts set on any one place; in truth, we're not knowledgeable enough to make such a choice. My wife has a few years left of teaching, but she can transfer to any in-state public school and retain her health care and retirement benefits. I'm self-employed. A small piece of land's end is what we're after, but it would be all right if it were in the vicinity of, say, historic Chestertown.

When the realtors have heard enough to supposedly figure us out (it takes ten minutes at the most), they tap the keyboards at their workstations. Printers go into paroxysms, spewing out photos in half-tones with arcanely abbreviated specifics. Dexterously collating the printouts, the realtors pass them across the desktops. We scan the harvest: most of the listings are out of our price range. Yet since we've traveled so far, and have such a long drive back, we ask if we can see one or two intriguing prospects just to get a feel for what's out there. "Why sure, how about right now?" The canny realtor is not about to pass up a jackpot commission from an impulse buyer. We clamber back into the car and, with the realtor leading the way, hit the home-hunting trail.

Embarking on these waterfront inspections gives K and me a romantic impetus. We loosen up; we become drifters as well as dreamers, and the more places we see, the more we're tempted to think of our finances as taffy—stretchable to any limit. It's fun to imagine settling down in one of the many mansions that always seem to be for sale (we speculate on why wealthy homeowners fold the tent with such frequency). Fortunately for us, experience doesn't let us dream too much or drift too far. In Kent County, where we buckle down to a serious search, we seek out one realtor in particular who seems to understand our budget restrictions, even as she succeeds in whetting our appetite.

She keeps up a litany about how the best properties often get snapped up as soon as they go on the market. She recommends against building a new house on waterfront—too many environmental regulations to deal with. She also reminds us that the surcharge for waterfront's elusive aesthetic advantage can be avoided if we settle for *waterview* instead. Since we don't need a dock per se, we could situate ourselves inland a bit (and if we acquire a larger boat in the future, we can always lease dock space at a marina). Should this idea appeal to us, she's prepared to show us some exclusive listings that are reasonably priced—properties that deliver, in her estimation, every penny of value, including swimming pool, hot tub, heat pump, double-glazed windows, professional landscaping, and two-car garage. Each of these homes faces water in one direction or another, but there's less wind and no erosion to worry about.

By now, we're well aware of the potential drawbacks of locating directly on a shoreline, but, for all her logic, we can't be swayed. The closer we are to the water, the more we like it. Nonplussed, she leads us to waterfront exclusives that are just beyond our can-do, as if to reprimand us for overreaching. "Remember," she says, "your first hundred thousand is not for the house or the lot but for that water border." Much of what she shows us is situated in subdivisions up one of the numerous creeks of the Chester River, or on the river itself, with a hundred feet or less of very shallow shoreline. Her point is well taken: it's all overpriced. In many cases, the artificiality of the land divisions looks just plain stupid. Despite the realtor's honeyed blather previewing the features she's sure we'll go gaga over, we find the properties to be only cookie-cutter replicas of one another. We spend several Saturdays inspecting, re-inspecting, and ultimately rejecting. We just don't want the home of our dreams to be in full view of another gray neo-post-Victorian saltbox with a pressure-treated deck fronting the phragmites.

Taking a breather from the realtor, my wife and I do some exploring on our own. In Betterton, a beach community in Cecil County, we stumble on a For Sale sign at the bottom of a driveway leading to a wooded bluff. Across the street, not a hundred feet away, are condominium apartments; down the block is a public picnic shelter and, in the other direction, an abandoned chapel. Beyond the bend of the driveway is a kind of primeval privacy, a shady hideaway that conceals a turn-of-the-century frame house in disrepair, with a fine, high view of the upper bay. *Eureka!* we exclaim, we've found it! The way the property slopes off into a wooded ravine to either side, with the condos fully obscured to the rear, makes it one in a million. Pleasure craft are plying the wide expanse of water and muffled explosions periodically concuss the air—we are directly across from the U.S. Army's Aberdeen Proving Ground.

We're propelled out of the been-there-done-that doldrums. The property's condition should ensure a bargain price—how could it be otherwise? The only serious drawback seems to be the house, all boarded up, impassive to our curiosity. As we walk around the neglected perimeter, I make a mental list of all that needs to be done: replace the roof and siding, modernize the windows, install patio doors, insulate, redo the plumbing and wiring. . . . My construction skills haven't been put to use in some time, but I haven't forgotten them. I can see myself taking on this project, if only for the privilege of looking out on this view.

The indicated realtor, seventeen miles to the north in Cecilton, is sitting at his desk on the mid-summer Saturday afternoon, bored. He sizes up our eager-beaverness through his trifocals. Ah, the property at Betterton, he says, the place with the splendid overlook on the bay. Yes, and seclusion, too. Wonderful old trees, including some mature hemlocks. The lot is choice as choice can be. Its asking price *was* $750,000, but as of last week it's not for sale anymore. He just hasn't gotten around to taking down the sign. As a matter of fact, *he* owns it, and he hates to be the bearer of bad tidings, but the house and all the trees are slated to be torn down in a couple of weeks. In their place will be erected—surprise, surprise—another condo complex.

My wife and I are terribly deflated by this news, but something is clear to us now: ideally, we'd like a place on the "big" water. From that day forward, we decide to narrow our search to bayfront only. We can't get over that wide and elevated westward view. And it wouldn't hurt to be a little closer to Chestertown in Kent County—and, come to think of it, not straight across from noisy Aberdeen.

Apprised of our redefined preference, our original realtor steers us to a listing in the Swan Creek area, a twenty-eight-acre "Nature lover's paradise" between paved road and shoreline and comprising, en route to its terminal bluff, four distinct ecosystems: a swamp, a forest, an open meadow, and a thicket. Located in the middle of the latter, wholly lacking a view of the water, is a farmhouse disfigured over the years by poorly carpentered additions. Barricaded by overgrowth, the house seems cut off from the world, an aspect we love, although, try as we might, we fail to see any redeeming qualities in the structure itself. The only solution—in accordance with county zoning regulations—would be to raze it and build a new house on the existing "footprint," or foundation. Among its least attractive qualities is a musty odor reminiscent of death—within the year, the owner had succumbed to cancer. A footpath through the briary tangle leads to where her ashes are buried on the bluff's edge, beside a tilted outhouse and a crude ladder descending the ten feet or so to the beach.

Intrigued, K and I revisit this property numerous times, exploring ways to tame it sufficiently for our use, despite the fact that its drawbacks are legion. Gypsy moths are killing the stateliest of the oaks; Virginia creeper, wild grape, and poison ivy are smothering all the other trees and bushes. In the house, asbestos is everywhere—the siding, the floor and ceiling tile, the chimney grouting, the pipe insulation. A detached garage, almost totally envined, is sheathed with flaking asbestos board. Just looking around makes us wish we had donned HazMat suits and were breathing through activated charcoal filters.

The owner's estate has set the price at $350,000, but the word is that they're eager to sell and will entertain all offers. Even if a low bid of half the asking price were accepted, though, we still might not be able to borrow the shortfall from a bank, because the place has liability written all over it. In addition to the teardown (the realtor thinks the local volunteer fire company can oblige us here) and the cost of new construction, the long gravel lane needs shoring up where it bisects the swamp. There might be some profit in logging the biggest trees, since they're dying anyway, but what about the vines? How will we ever conquer them? There's no point in cutting them back, since they'll just regrow tenfold. Bulldozing or all-out chemical warfare seem to be the only options, but we're repulsed at the thought.

So we dither. No, it's impossible. Wait, maybe it just *might* be possible. We're smitten by the Edenic aspect, the pellmell photo-synthesis in hummocks and swags festooning every branch and bough. Soughing wind and birdsong weave an impenetrable screen of privacy. One afternoon we thread our way to the over-grown apple orchard and make love on a plush bed of moss. Rabbits teem in the underbrush and, judging by the droppings, so do deer. The realtor has said something about bald eagles in the vicinity, and when we see our first soaring pair, we're rendered speechless by their majesty.

For contrast, and to keep our sense of proportion, we look at two or three other properties in the same price range, but they don't hold a candle to this one, one-of-a-kind-wise. We're on the verge of committing ourselves to a contract, but something holds us back. Do we really want, much less need, our very own nature preserve? K reminds me that I'm not as young as I used to be, nor is she. A project like this could go on forever, but maybe that's the beauty of it. We debate the pros and cons, unable to make up our minds.

To resolve the dilemma, we agree to have one last look. The August morning, already stifling by the time we cross the bay, is off to a crawling start with the Route 213 bottlenecks through Centreville and Chestertown. Arriving at the property, we reluc-tantly leave the air-conditioned car for the insect-buzzing merid-ian blaze. Our plan, to walk the boundary of the twenty-eight acres, rapidly turns into a hardship hike. More than once, I wish I had a machete. Deep into the forested section, we are disheart-ened to find hunters' tree stands—my wife counts nine of them—and two, heretofore unseen, are less than twenty feet from the lane we'd be driving several times a day. We picture ourselves dodging bullets from inebriated hunters. Later, we even discover a couple of ladders sequestered in the bushes.

The tree stands, plus the duck blinds in the swamp, cast the property in a different light. This place is a hunting ground, and has been so for untold decades. *It's not meant for us to live in the middle of.* Overheated and itching, we cut across to the potholed lane and head for the car. That evening, back in Greenbelt, a strong allergic reaction hits me. It must have been something I came in contact with, but whether animal, vegetable, or mineral, I haven't a clue. I'm in such bad shape, feverish and swollen, that K insists on driving me to the emergency room, where a doctor examines me and puts me on steroids.

The real-estate search is on hold while I recuperate, and for a few weeks afterward, we try not to think about Chesapeake Bay or the Eastern Shore. Needless to say, putting them out of our minds is infeasible; by mid-October, we're crossing over the bridge again. The realtor has expected us back all along, and she briefs us on a brand-new listing: a house in the bayfront hamlet of Tolchester.

We've been through Tolchester several times and haven't been particularly impressed with the place. It's a motley unincorporated community, a place with a past far more remarkable than its present. There was once an amusement park in Tolchester—actually, it was *the* premier excursion park on the Chesapeake for more than eighty years. Steamboats from Baltimore carried thousands of visitors daily in season. After World War II, the park fell into permanent decline, accelerated in 1952 with the opening of the initial span of the Bay Bridge. By 1962, outmoded, underattended, in dire need of maintenance, and deep in red ink, the park closed for good.

Although every trace of Tolchester's former attraction is gone—including the pavilion and roller coaster and grand hotel—the surrounding subdivision, Tolchester Estates, dating from the 1920s, lives on, albeit forlornly. Many of the streets, named after states, are little more than unused rights-of-way. New York Avenue, for example, peters out in the vicinity of a rusted fifty-five-gallon drum. One-story bungalows, some telescoped with added bedrooms and porches, sit on nondescript lots demarcated by storage sheds and backyard barbecues. Boats on trailers take up much of the driveway space. The community has no street lamps, just a catenary of utility poles and overhead wires. Waterfront homes are among the tidiest—with manicured hedges, brimming flowerboxes, ornamental grasses—and next best kept are the waterviews east of Bayview Avenue; then toward the cornfields behind them are the landscapeless dwellings of the shade tree mechanics. Vacant lots remain vacant. This is not a locale of upscale appeal, but rather a quiet convergence of permanent baycombers and part-timers, many of whom are retired. To call it a resort (as the realtor did at first) is a misnomer; rather, call it a gridded periphery of a landmark that is no more. No two houses are alike, no two dogs are alike, and no one dog is trammeled by anything as restrictive as a leash.

In the mid-1950s, a Nike surface-to-air missile base was established next door. Its mission was to protect Washington, D.C., and Baltimore from Soviet bomber attacks—this before the days of prairie- and ocean-hidden ICBMs. A battery of four aboveground launching platforms stood not far inside a barbed-wire-topped chain link fence along the central thoroughfare. The missile platforms are still there, spiderlike anomalies rising from the weeds, as are the support and fueling facilities, barracks and mess hall—all flat-roofed, cinder-block one-story structures, very plain and fiftyish, eminently expendable in the event of their being caught at ground zero. The fence, rusty and honeysuckle entwined, is also extant, with an entrance gate and guard house that look quaint by today's military security standards. The base was deactivated in 1973; today, it is best characterized as a swords-to-plowshares phenomenon, having become the site of the annual Kent County Agricultural Fair, with corn and milo raised in its extremities. Year round, a catering business leases the mess hall.

Into this somewhat reclusive community with its best, or at least busiest years behind it, we drive, while the realtor keeps up a running commentary about price comparisons and nearness to shopping areas. Chestertown is eleven miles to the northeast, a straightforward two-road connection; Rock Hall is five miles to the south. An 1814 battle of the War of 1812 was fought at nearby Caulk's Field.[1] Good schools, several denominations of churches, reasonable taxes, a recorded history that goes back to the pre-colonial era—painstakingly, the realtor enumerates the selling points. As she speaks, the sparkling blue-gray of the Chesapeake Bay makes its first appearance at the end of an empty street. My wife and I are chauffeured straight through to the farthest extreme of the subdivision, where the pavement turns to gravel and zigzags through a brambly woods. We are not far from the edge of what is known as Mitchell's Bluff. All at once, we apprise the object of our journey: a tree-sheltered four-part white house with a green roof. We have arrived. Just beyond, and forty feet below, purls the quick bay surf, and, on the distant horizon, behind the mauve line of the Western Shore, are the barely perceptible skyscrapers of Baltimore and Towson. It is a location to die for.

For some reason, my first thought focuses on the green shingles. Stereotypical prospective buyer that I am, I see the trees, not the forest. Noting that the shingles will need replacing in ten years or so, I remind K not to overlook any of the property's other flaws, nor be overly swayed by the—in realty parlance—gorgeous setting.

The original part of the house, a bow-windowed cinderblock summer bungalow dating from 1949, with a fireplace and a sleeping attic, has been added to, twice on the left and twice on the right. On the left, a kitchen no bigger than a boat's galley was later expanded with a two-steps-down glassed-in atrium (moisture-trapped thermopane, I note with dismay); on the right, a bedroom wing with another bow window, and then a recently built two-story mother-in-law addition, with its own kitchenette, upper and lower bathrooms, and spiral staircase. The resultant agglomeration, unified on the outside in vinyl lap siding and polymer shutters (green) that bracket the fenestration, can vaguely be described as "Cape Cod style," but would better be termed a sum total of add-ons, a long and narrow structure with

five inconsistent roof lines and, in its ground-floor rooms, re-
mainders of once-exterior windows transformed into bookcases.

The house stands at the center of a wind-trimmed grove of
sassafras, holly, and dogwood, with additional loblolly pine, locust, cedar, and Kentucky coffee that fulfilled some long-ago
landscaper's plan—a setting the agent's brochure terms "park-
like." Sourly, I see it as a lawn mower's nightmare. Two hip-
roofed outbuildings, the manufactured kind skidded off flatbed
trucks, flank at right angles—one behind the kitchen, the other
beside the two-story addition. The edge of the bluff, not ten yards
away, slopes off in honeysuckle and crown vetch, and treelings
have gained toeholds on its bank as well. A set of wooden steps
leads down to the water, where a fishing dock thrusts out from
the bulkheading over a boulder pile. All three hundred feet of
the lot's water frontage have been rip-rapped—that is to say,
buttressed with a mounded seawall of quarried boulders. Water
sloshes between the bottommost rocks, darkly wetting the inter-
stices, and on closer inspection, I note that the tides have
jammed in all manner of flotsam.

On this first visit, the sellers happen to be at home. The husband, a pleasant fellow in his early sixties, prefers that he, not
the realtor, show me around (his wife similarly conducts K).

"How can you bear to be leaving a place like this?" I ask—as
foolish a question as any potential buyer ever asked a seller, a
giveaway of infatuation.

"Retiring. And high time."

I inquire about the danger of the bluff being washed away in a
storm and the house falling into the bay. "There's no chance of
that ever happening," the husband says, explaining about the
eighty-four truckloads of rock that constitute the bulkheading.
A ramp was cut through the bluff on the adjoining vacant lot—
with that owner's permission—so that the trucks could dump
the rocks right where they were needed, at which point a loader
piled them even higher. The rocks top off at six feet above mean
high tide. When the job was finished, the bluff was restored.

It becomes obvious that our host is warming to one of his favorite topics. The house is now safe for at least a hundred years,
he avows, but the erosion has been checked none too soon.
According to a lawn maintenance person who worked for the
previous owner, the distance from foundation to bluff edge is
half of what it used to be in the 1960s. Storms, wave action from
the shipping channel—he points to the red and green buoys three
hundred yards or so offshore—freezing and thawing, plus the
incremental rise of sea level are all contributing to the bluff's
demise. Rip-rapped, the property is protected, but the adjacent
lot, with an equal amount of frontage, is another story. It should
have been rip-rapped at the same time, but the absentee owner, a
man in his nineties—and, interestingly, one of the surveyors of
the original Tolchester Estates subdivision—wouldn't undertake
the expense. The husband concedes that the old man had a
point: why pile up all those rocks when there's no house? Not in
three lifetimes will that enormous cliff be totally undercut;
meanwhile, it comprises, above, a flat greensward (that he, being
the good neighbor, voluntarily mows) and, below, a swimmable
beach.

The checkered flag of hopefulness flashes in my brain. What if
my wife and I make an offer on both the sellers' home and the
adjacent lot? By doing so, we can get twice the frontage and a
good measure of additional privacy, since the vacant lot stretches
to the wooded tract that visually cuts off the rest of the community. (There is one house on a large estate further along the lane,
well concealed by trees.) Most likely, the lot itself isn't buildable, that is, it's no longer deep enough for the hundred-foot
coastal setback required of new construction under the present
zoning ordinance. Still, that's not to say it couldn't be lived on.
Mentally, I summon up a loud family spending the summer next
door in a pop-up camper.

As if reading my mind, the husband mentions that the lot just
might be for sale. Nobody has ever camped there during the time
he and his wife have lived beside it, but that doesn't mean nobody ever will. He'll be happy to approach the old man person-

ally, acting as sole agent for the transaction. He relates to me
how the former surveyor has an intense dislike for lawyers and
realtors. Not many years ago, in a similar situation, the old man
sold another property[2] to a straw agent, and it turned out that
the real buyer was a longstanding personal enemy. The mistake
will never be repeated. Although his three hundred feet of bluff
and beach may have passed from buildable to non-buildable status, it'll never be publicly offered for sale. But now, in advanced
age, he might be amenable to parting with it, especially if he
knew it would be joined with his neighbors' lot, the folks who
have taken such good care of his own.

So, after a prolonged inspection inside and outside and under
the house in the crawl space, followed by deliberations that
cover every conceivable angle we can think of and then some, K
and I decide to take the plunge. Our financial resources are
no match for the outlay, but it's now or never. We're convinced
that the property's one-of-a-kind appeal won't remain unnoticed
for long. A contract is duly drawn up with an offer, significantly
below asking price and contingent on the acquisition of the
lot next door. All we can do is cross our fingers and wait for a
response.

The wait is a short one, less than forty-eight hours. The old
man approves the lot sale on our terms. Our evanescent notions
turn substantive as the sellers bump down the asking price and
we ante up the bid. Climbing into the fiscal stratosphere, we
hang on, hoping that the latest thousand-dollar increment will
be the last. At an impasse, the husband and wife offer owner fi-
nancing at 7 percent, thus removing the biggest stumbling block,
the fact that we can't qualify for a king-size bank mortgage. Two
family members sympathetic to our cause proffer additional
short-term loans. Cumbersome as a blue heron, the deal finally
gets off the ground, just short of the stall point for both parties.

They move out and we move in. K and I are exhausted, ex-
cited beyond belief, in debt deeper than we had thought work-
able, and apprehensive as hell about the future. We're cranking
up at a time when most of our contemporaries are thinking

about winding down. We're putting our kids, half in and half out of the nest, through the hurdle of acclimatizing themselves to yet another parental domicile. We're bidding adieu to people and places we'll never be on quotidian terms with again, trading the familiar for the unknown. It's odd to be plunked down where otherwise we'd continue to be wide-eyed tourists just passing through. The day trips are over. For better or for worse, we are one with the Chesapeake. Henceforth, every sunset we gaze upon will spread beyond the distant horizon that nurtured the life we left behind.

chapter
2

Roughly four hundred square miles of water lie within the view from Mitchell's Bluff. The western shore stretches for almost fifty miles, concealed toward the north by the nearer Pooles Island, which is part of Aberdeen Proving Ground, then reappearing at the Susquehanna National Wildlife Refuge.

From left to right, with the naked eye, we can pick out the U.S. Navy's communications array south of Annapolis, the anomalous Mt. Carmel, the smokestacks of Baltimore Gas and Electric's Wagner and Brandon Shores plants, the shipyard and steelworks at Sparrows Point, the hulking "portainer" cranes at Seagirt and Dundalk, the Francis Scott Key Bridge (over the Patapsco), Baltimore, the dredged ramparts of Hart-Miller Island, the beacon offshore from Bowleys Quarters, Towson, the Carroll Island generating station, and Aberdeen's water tower.

Greater than a backdrop, the voluminous sky absorbs—*cushions* may be a better word—every reflection and refraction of the watery flatness. It is a painter's sky, a treasury of light even on the grayest of days, so vast as to leave the sliver of distant shoreline in the lurch of inconsequence. The totality can be, at times, almost too much to take in. Facing such unalloyed dramatic intensity calls for, at the very least, a kind of emotional fortitude. Dawn and sunset can knock one's socks off, fog nearly suffocates, midday bears down like a boot heel.

Under these conditions, looking becomes more of a compulsion than a pastime. The view can be likened to a four-dimensional palette constantly refreshed with sensation. Colorwise, blue serves as the predominant hue, but gray, pink, yellow, mauve, lavender, chartreuse, and amber play supporting roles. Weather is writ large as whole systems and fronts gather beyond the horizon, then make their splayed approach, stalling or passing over. Distant squalls, vertically striated like stage curtains, burnish far-off water with pewter; then, as the pressure system moves east, the waves here turn into insistent shore-knockers sent to sell the Encyclopedia of Time. Severe weather occurs in black and white, the wind battering horizontally at first, followed by rain's head-on collision.

Every hour, the weather rules rewrite themselves. An oncoming strato-cumulus cloudbank can be a sheltering blanket or a flattening steamroller. With no warning, a breeze picks up or dies. It is impossible to forecast gradation and duration. Unexpected beatitudes result from the meteorological inconsistency: the snarl of a storm becomes the smile of a cloud-scudded day. On other occasions, the entire four-hundred-mile expanse can be as placid as a millpond.

Above the western shore, a strip of sulphur dioxide often wafts like a long mustard pillow—a pillow on top of the head rather than underneath it. Even at so great a distance, the inversion gives pause: all those cars and trucks and lawnmowers, all those chemical processes, all those people. The tall stacks spew their patently obvious contribution—yes, and we're diametrically downwind—but there's a continent behind the scene. Greater environmental thinkers than I have calculated how many tens of thousands of tons of industrial filth are annually bequeathed to the sky above Chesapeake Bay. Sometimes, I can't help but feel I'm staring straight at a strong economy's legacy—inhaling it, exhaling it. And at night, greater Baltimore throws off mercury/ sodium vapor in an orangey glow, rendered all the more intense as it bounces streetward again from the clouds.

In spite of all this, there is atmospheric clarity, seemingly paradoxical in an age when air pollution's obfuscation is the norm. In fact, the due-west exposure here showcases the sun's diurnal journey with optimal illustration. In the pink of early morning, the water surface dances violetly as white workboats, now rose-colored, ply the crab buoy fields. As the sun approaches its zenith, the light becomes so keen, so palpable that I'm inspired to get busy in the studio. By late afternoon the brightness, tinged with gold, languishes as the sun hangs foursquare over the water and in the eyes, extending the shadows behind me even as it extends my chores left undone. And then blooms sunset: that reenergizing bromide, Nature's passionate production, affecting the water as much as the sky. It announces that all work must be laid down, and perhaps glasses (or bottles) raised. K and I repair to our slatted bench on the bluff and gape. And this is not to diminish that later sparkling straightaway, the moonbeam, which gilds the dark bay and makes us wonder why people rarely enjoy the night for its own sake anymore.

I describe all the above by way of overview, a generalist's approach to an everchanging spectacle. But there is so much more to observe in detail that it really helps to use binoculars. My old pair has become indispensible; I like to know exactly where they are, if they're not hanging from a strap around my neck. Even when not using them, I carry them with me from room to room against the likelihood that something of note will appear shortly through the bay-facing windows.

I acquired them many years ago, back when I had no real reason to use binoculars on a daily, or even a monthly basis. I wasn't into bird-, sport-, or plane-watching, and I wasn't spying on anybody either. I just liked the idea of having them at the ready. For want of a better place, I stowed them in the glove compartment of my car, against the express instructions of the manufacturer, which stated that this was the absolutely worst place to keep a precision optical instrument. I figured I'd spot something worthy of closer inspection most likely along a highway—a highway, in all probability, far from home.

Birdwatching is the first and perhaps best use of the old binoculars these days. In residence or migration are incredible numbers of wild ducks and geese, as well as swans, hawks, vultures, seagulls, ospreys, eagles, kingfishers, herons, and a host of common, and not so common, songbirds. A new sighting—visual clue plus signature honk, trill, chirp, or squawk—almost always occasions a nomenclatural treasure hunt, sending us thumbing through the dog-eared *Peterson's* for an illustrated likeness.

Fall is the best season for bay birding. Close by the house, we watch for iridescent flocks of European starlings, not particularly thrilling as individuals—homely, in fact—but they do create unusual moiré effects in multitudes. Waxwings, cardinals, flickers, and woodpeckers are glimpsed in various deciduous arbors. Warblers and sparrows can be found in the bluff-edge brush, while mourning doves monopolize the utility wires. High over the water soar the large birds of prey, and carrion pickers glide above the beach. Pointy-winged gulls manage to insinuate themselves everywhere, as do ducks. Cormorants and mallards float singly or in concert, gun-shy Brandts and canvasbacks barrel along as fast as they can beat their scaredy-cat pinions. North to south, formations of Canada geese obstreperously file to wherever it is they're going, a collective brouhaha that announces their passage for miles. Snow geese travel more deliberately, in exquisite echelon. Far in the distance, bridging for long minutes the expanse of the bay itself, thousands of specks in undulating, multi-stranded streams flow against the wind. Only with the aid of the binoculars can we confirm that the particles are indeed birds. Perhaps millions should be substituted for thousands; the first time I witness a migration of this magnitude, I realize I'm looking at more birds than I've seen collectively in my entire life. I'm reminded of nineteenth-century eyewitness accounts of skies blackened with passenger pigeons, prairies carpeted with buffalo. The unidentifiable streams are winging toward a southwestern wintering ground—a mass exodus on an interstate flyway.

The scope of Nature's intrinsic sky traffic is almost incomprehensible, and were it not for the opacity of the bay itself, a similar observation might be made about its submarine dimension. Birds (and people) that fish give testimony to all that teems within. Trying to make out what they spot beneath the water's surface, I train my binoculars on the trajectories of ospreys and eagles as they drop toward their prey. Alas, I see only the birds' determination. I've had to content myself with an excellent, though out-of-print, memoir, Gilbert Klingel's *The Bay: A Naturalist Discovers a Universe of Life Above and Below the Chesapeake* (Dodd, Mead & Co., New York, 1951), in which the author describes how, supplied with air hose and flashlight, he stood on the bay bottom at various locations and observed the creatures that passed by. I won't be duplicating his feat any time soon. No naturalist, I show little patience for codification and scientific method. Moreover, I have a low tolerance for discomfort in the pursuit of empirical observation (wearing a primitive diving helmet, Klingel sometimes stood transfixed underwater until he was thoroughly chilled; at other times, he crouched in the cramped quarters of a homemade diving chamber).

But I, too, know what it means to be transfixed. On the breezy bluff, watchfulness has become my métier. I can't help but react to this abundantly stimulating setting. There's too much to miss, so why miss any of it at all? When an interesting bird flies past, I'm *there*, swinging lens to eye. "Wow, look at that!" I'll exclaim, if my wife hasn't already exclaimed at it first.

Yet the real reason I'll never be a bona fide naturalist is that I'm too interested in *un*natural things. Between water and sky, I can pretty much gorge myself on everything else that floats and flies. When training jets from Dover Air Force Base scream overhead, I rush outside (but they're gone in a matter of seconds). Ditto for the Coast Guard helicopters that patrol low along the coast. Similarly, I'll watch slow-poke jetliners descend toward Baltimore-Washington International Airport, some twenty-five miles away, and marvel at the relativity of speed and distance. At any given moment, day or night, there are probably ten airplanes visible in the sky—visible, that is, to the not-so-naked eye. Also, I keep a lookout to the north for the occasional (conventional, thank heavens!) mushroom cloud rising from Aberdeen. I can even anticipate, ten or twelve seconds later, the thump of the shock-wave.

Offshore, green and red buoys demarcate the route of the

container ships, the roll-on roll-off car carriers (called *ro-ros*), the bulk and break-bulk freighters, plus the bay's astounding variety of tugs and barges. This shipping traffic moves to and from marine terminals to the north in Wilmington and Philadelphia, and to the south in Baltimore and Norfolk. As the channel enters the northern, or upper, bay, it approaches and runs close to the shoreline at Tolchester, paralleling an underwater formation known as Mitchell's Ledge, which is about fifteen feet deep on average. Maintained by private contractors for the U.S. Army Corps of Engineers, the channel needs to stay at least thirty-five feet deep and six hundred feet wide as it continues through the series of turns marked by the lighted buoys. Red #32, at about the latitude of our house, signifies a 10-degree rudder to port on the northward journey to the Chesapeake & Delaware Canal.

Close-up—through the binoculars, that is—the oceangoing merchant vessels are fascinating. They bear little resemblance to the freighters and tankers I remember as a boy, and later as a sailor in the U.S. Navy. In addition to their increased tonnage and bulbously undershot bows, today's vessels are cargo specific to the point where their function truly dictates their form. A car carrier, for instance, is essentially a floating parking garage, its superstructure extending from stem to stern and its beam as broad as a flattop's. Three thousand automobiles fit within, parked bumper to bumper on decks just tall enough for roof clearance. Loading and unloading is usually facilitated by an off-set ramp at the stern (for mooring parallel to a pier) that is raised above the asymmetrical fantail when the ship is underway. The ships' names and flags of registry raise my global consciousness. In several weeks' viewing, I amass the following sample:

> *Harmony Ace*—Hong Kong
> *CCNI Anakena*—Hamburg
> *Arktis Crystal*—København
> *Petrobulk Power*—Nassau
> *Hoegh Dyke*—George Town, Cayman Is.
> *Synnøve Knutsen*—Haugesund

Century Leader No. 3—Tokyo
Olivebank—Panama
Lucky River—Panama
Gypsum Baron—Hamilton
MSC Stefania—Panama
Villach—Limassol
Icaria D.—Napoli
Skødsborg—Rungstad
Stolt Avance—Monrovia
MSC Mirella—Panama
CSAV Ranquil—St. Johns
Sunbelt Dixie—Monrovia
Schakenborg—Rungsted
Figaro—Stockholm
Seabulk Magnachem—Port Everglades FL
Mercury Ace—Osaka
Asphalt Champion—Piraeus

At most ports of delivery, exportable goods are waiting to be shipped abroad. Few of the oceangoing vessels appear to be riding empty, regardless of the direction they're headed. Worldwide commerce, spread among approximately 38,000 deep-draft hulls—or *bottoms*, in ship lingo—is going strong, although not strong enough to usher in the futuristic fleet that has been on the visionaries' drawing boards for the past twenty years. Much of the present merchant fleet, for all its design efficiency, is most definitely aging. Through the binoculars, I detect tell-tale defects: buckling plates, dents and scrapes, rust. A Russian freighter—not mentioned in my sample because I couldn't translate the Cyrillic—steamed by so noisily that it seemed on the verge of conking out. Another ship, of Liberian registry, looked as if it had been scorched by a fire. Some ships pass whose fores and afts don't quite match up, hull sections cobbled together from previous incarnations. Other vessels look almost ready for the shipbreakers. The most obvious indicator of shipshapeness in an aging vessel, aside from its general seaworthiness, is the paint job on its superstructure, for this is the area that's easiest to maintain. The hull can (and often does) look ratty, but the part above gleams. As a former enlisted man who did plenty of chipping and red-leading, I can attest to the pride that comes from such work: when the superstructure is "squared away," a sailor has faith in the old tub.

True, these ships don't steam along Chesapeake Bay for the purpose of being stared at, but by dint of their proximity, their passage is an event in itself. Although they proceed—with pilots—at quarter speed, their bow and wake waves hit shore within minutes, upsetting the normal lapping equilibrium and constituting a disturbance that I exonerate as a byproduct of the balance of trade between nations. Prior to living in Tolchester, I didn't give much thought to the fact that so many consumer goods sold in the United States are manufactured on the other side of the world. How do they get here? Take a look off the bluff.

Shipping containers, those twenty- and forty-foot-long, vertically corrugated boxes stacked and secured on cargo decks (more are in holds) are the standard into which nearly everything except cars and heavy equipment fits. Fully loaded container ships have a decidedly topheavy appearance—with a navigation view, no doubt, barely over the topmost box—but they ply the channel safely above the Plimsoll, or load line, mark, with cargo to be distributed, even as more is lifted aboard, at the next port of call.

Bulk carriers of raw materials such as bauxite, gypsum, coal, and grain are impressive in their own right. Cargo is confined beneath an array of hatches and slewing booms or conveyor belts. The sweeping hulls are shorn of all other vertical protuberances, making them seem inordinately long. Liquid and liquified gas carriers, with their low freeboard, wellheads, pumps, and firefighting stations, likewise strike the imagination. About the only ships that don't pass by, due to the draft limitations of the channel and the narrow canal to the north, are supertankers (Very Large Crude Carriers, or VLCCs); however, many millions of barrels of bulk fuel are conveyed past our house in coastal tankers and barges en route to and from the refineries of Wilmington and Philadelphia.

A world-circumnavigating 20,000-gross-ton vessel represents, both in itself and in its cargo, the convergence of many arts and technologies plus the investment of tens of millions of dollars. Knowing, as I do, next to nothing about the mechanics of propulsion and navigation, not to mention the cross-currents of global trade, I peer through the binoculars and develop a kind of yearning. If I could be a very temporary stowaway on one ship, boarding it at Dundalk, say, and spending an hour breathing the belowdecks aroma and feeling the engine-room vibration through the soles of my shoes, then I could be put ashore with the Maryland pilot, at the eastern end of the C&D Canal before heading into the Delaware Bay, and, if lucky, thumb a ride home.

Tugboats factor in my bayfaring fantasies, too. I could probably get a trip aboard one if I pulled the right strings. There's something lovable about these snub-nosed, exhaust-spewing mules of the bay. Their muscular upsweptness of curvate bulwark fendered with old tires conveys a certain déclassé appeal. A tugboat at work is a sure sign that all is well on the water, and when a tugboat is underway by itself, unencumbered after, or headed toward, a delivery, it can be downright picturesque, like a road tractor without a trailer. I wonder if there's such a thing as an old tug nobody wants? Such a vessel might make perfect retirement quarters for K and me, and even earn us a little income on the side.

At times I regret arriving on the Chesapeake too late to have seen the bay steamers, the bugeyes and log canoes, the skipjack fleets that abounded earlier in the century. Occasionally, a restored skipjack on a day charter will sail past, conspicuous with raked mast and overweening equilateral canvas and crewed with paying customers. The lore of the old oyster dredgers is extensive, but the fleet is nearly extinct (according to the latest reports, it's at ten boats and dropping). Today's watermen continue to eke out a sustenance via that other formerly great industry of the bay, crabbing. I watch the rubber-gloved-and-aproned men in their no-frills workboats, puttering not far offshore. Through the binoculars, I can plainly see that gaffing, hauling up, emptying, and re-baiting scores of crab pots one by one is tedious physical work—and hardly a get-rich-quick scheme—but I know also that there's less labor involved now than there used to be. For one thing, the catch is only a fraction of its former size. For another, today's workboats are fast and maneuverable, constructed of fiberglass and equipped with the latest in marine amenities. The watermen will stay out all day, covering miles of territory dotted with their individually painted buoys. As crabbing season ends, a few of the boats still meander on the margins, jury-rigged with tarpaulin and side flaps to cut the wind, the crew checking a few pots but mostly fishing for perch. In December, boats can be seen floating together in twos and threes, the watermen smoking cigarettes, passing around a bottle, shooting the breeze. I suspect the men who go out on the raw chilly days do so not because they have to, but because they want to—that, or their significant others have banished them till suppertime.

Pleasure boats glide past few and far between during the winter months, but in warmer weather they're in abundance. Increasingly popular, too, are offshore performance craft, otherwise known as "cigarette boats," aquadynamic monsters with extended snouts, wraparound windshields, and sunpads over their engine compartments. Clapping the water, they hurtle along at speeds up to sixty miles an hour, often in schools of three or more. When the entire expanse reverberates with their wide-open hedonism, I feel as though I belong on another planet. Speed isn't my guiding principle, nor acceleration my watchword. Far out on the bay, their racing would appear smooth and easy, but through the binoculars I extrapolate the brutal propulsion, the searing splash and tearing wind. They call this *fun*?

I would prefer passage in one of those *real* yachts, playthings of the affluent that voyage up and down the Inland Waterway or magisterially set a course for the Bahamas. A really big cabin cruiser, one that's fabulously expensive to own and maintain—

and well-provisioned to boot—is my idea of a status symbol (yes, I'd make a fine Chesapeake Brahmin if I were given half the chance). I can picture myself relaxing on deck, Bloody Mary in hand, contributing to a high-minded conversation, while a hired captain busies himself with the navigation and a steward sees to the refilling of my glass. I especially relate to vintage boats with plenty of brightwork and mahogany trim.

From the bluff, I'm becoming something of an armchair expert on the difference between old and new money afloat. Old money is comfortable in a graceful yacht with a little age on it, while new money prefers pizzazz—something white and ultra-sleek with a sinister James Bond look, black windows, and a forward-pricking prow. Old money is satisfied with a fluttering club burgee and a gold script moniker on the fantail: *Go Go*, *Joy Toy*, *Sea Wiz*. New money wants a swept-back flying bridge, a spate of portholes along the waterline, and more of a New Age twist to the portmanteau: *MoonSong*, *FireSprite*, *SprayScraper*. Still, new or old, they can invite me aboard any time.

The more modest cabin cruisers and fishing boats don't capture my attention nearly as much, for I find the majority generic-looking and ill-proportioned. Most are too squat, too wide, too tall. Their whip antennae stick up too high, their bow pulpits project out too far, and their cockpit canopies give them a top-heavy appearance. While proceeding at creditable rates of speed, they guzzle fuel, I'm told. Although I fully realize they're roomy, stable, and comfortable, I'll never want to own one. I'd sooner go all the way in stodginess and get a houseboat or one of those cute tugs—something different.

But I *am* intrigued by sailboats, short or long, plain or fancy. The idea of harnessing wind power has always appealed to me; this explains why, many years ago, I rigged up the canoe for sailing. Today, whenever I see sails out on the bay, I vicariously experience the tacking and jibing, the hiking out and hauling close to the wind. It thrills me to watch spinnakers grabbing bellyfuls of breeze. The fuller the sail, the more fun for the sailor. I even get a kick out of regattas along the Western Shore, a heat-distorted flock of handkerchiefs, so far away that the binoculars flatten three dimensions to two.

I often imagine the sail-cruising life, the mornings and after-noons of sun and bluster, and then, as the glowing ball sinks low, a placid anchorage up a protected cove, or a berth at a marina where there are neighbors to gab with and shore power to watch television by. One afternoon, however, my bubble bursts when I witness firsthand a sail cruise that is not so idyllic. While mowing the grass, I notice an aluminum mast sticking up, and on it, a slapping halyard. My first concern is that a sailboat's in trouble—it must have run aground. But stepping to the edge for a closer look, I find that the tide is in and the boat is very much afloat, a trim thirty-footer, with sails furled and an anchor line angled from the bow. Will it be staying for the night? It's all right with us if it does.

Binoculars raised, I observe the sailors, a sixtyish gent and his lady, both puffily attired in windbreakers. By their dour expressions, it appears that they're having a bad day. Also, they're both drinking. He keeps dodging in and out of the cabin—he must be attending to a malfunction of some sort—and she's clearly miffed at their predicament. I can't quite make out his words, but I surmise that he's cussing a blue streak and berating her, and she's responding with a kind of slow-mo malice that implies she wishes he were dead. Every time he ducks under the hatch, he bumps his head, and that sets him off again. Tumbler in hand and propped upon her cockpit cushion, she's staring stonily at the bay, doing her best to ignore him.

Eventually, he gets the engine started and returns to the helm to aim the craft away from land. Then he remembers the anchor, so he orders her to hold the wheel—"No, not that way, god-dammit, *this* way!" (here I can read his lips). Oblivious, she's steering for the beach. He jerks the wheel out of her hands and resets the course, then lurches to the foredeck, where he besot-tedly hauls in the Danforth anchor, banging it on the fiberglass (this I hear, and, enhanced as my vision is, I can even make out the gouges in the gelcoat). I lower the binoculars when the couple is safely away from the coastline. Evidently, neither he nor she is sober enough to raise the sail.

What else do I see? People fishing in open boats, spending whole days at it, bobbing and baking in the sun. During rockfish (striped bass) season, all manner of craft ride at anchor, as though in a watery parking lot, off Pooles Island and other hotspots where the upper bay's prime gamefish are known to be biting. Every few weeks in good weather, a flotilla of YPs (Yard Patrols, or training vessels from the U.S. Naval Academy, about the size and vintage of minesweepers) steams up the channel and back. In late fall and again in late winter, the Coast Guard cutter *Red Birch* comes by to change the channel buoys. Winter ice buoys are sleeker in profile, primary battery-driven instead of solar-powered, less prone to damage from the shifting floes. Also by way of channel maintenance, two Great Lakes Dredging Co. platforms operate in tandem at various locations yearlong. The derrick-hoisted clamshell buckets, sluicing muddy water through their iron jaws, drop load after load of silt onto waiting barges — a logistically complex procedure that continues around the clock in rotating shifts. Barges thus filled with dredging spoils are ferried, via tugs, to dumping sites such as Hart-Miller Island and Cox Creek. Meanwhile, the red-hulled scouting boat *Brazos River* probes, with its underwater scanners, for new places to be widened and deepened.

Sometimes I wonder if these boaters and skippers and pilots and deckhands bother to look around—perhaps even in our direction—with the selfsame intensity. I once watched a guy standing against the wheelhouse of a tugboat, seemingly staring straight back at me, but when I raised the binoculars, I saw that he was merely taking a piss over the side. And what about the people who dwell on the Western Shore, and the ones who work in the office towers and industrial plants that jut against the far horizon—are any of those folks actively monitoring what's going on? Or is everybody just too busy?

Jumping up to "go have a look" is a normal part of daily activity here, but my wife and I are aware that we're a distinct minority. Scrutinizing the passing scene has become old-fashioned, a luxury of spare time, which is in itself a luxury these days. In the not-too-distant future, we may even acquire a spotting scope on a tripod, to bring the goings-on even closer.

chapter

3

The wooden steps that descend unevenly through a cut in the bluff give the impression, from the top, of marching straight down and into the bay. Alongside lies the waste pipe from the water softener, which causes ground softening in the area immediately below the bottommost step, where six concrete patio stones have been placed to provide footing. The stones tend to slip in the mud when a person's full weight is upon them, but fortunately there's a railing to hang onto. I have no desire to improve this upon arrangement. My rationale goes something like this: the trouble it takes to descend cautiously makes the arrival at the bottom all the more worthwhile.

The bottom, in this instance, is a narrow ledge shored up with pressure-treated timbers and filter cloth, additionally buttressed by heaped boulders. This constitutes the smallest portion of the property, a caesura between bluff top and bay that is also the key to the house's survival. The water lies six to eight feet below, depending on the tide. Thirty feet to the right, through-bolted to the bulkhead, sits the rear edge of the fishing deck; farther to the right is the unrigged, upside-down canoe, chained to the trunk of a young locust.

By clambering leftward over the rip-rap, taking care not to slip or twist an ankle, I can set foot on the low-tide beach—low-tide because otherwise the choicest boulders for stepping are submerged. I have considered making the passage easier, weighed the pros and cons of erecting a catwalk of two-by-sixes over the rip-rap, but unless that walkway were placed unduly high, with extravagant underpinning, it wouldn't last through one bad storm.

Adding to the bludgeoning power of waves, all manner of heavy flotsam drifts in—logs, planks, whole trees even—and in the fury of a nor'easter these are tossed onto the rocks. My walkway would soon be reduced to matchsticks, and my practical nature would be forever reminding my visionary side, "I told you so."

The unprotected beach at the base of the bluff begins where the coarse polyhedral interlocking of the granite boulders ends, and continues some four hundred fifty feet to the nearest neighbor's bulkheading. What washes up on the pebbly sand can stay for hours or months, depending on specific gravity, anchoring characteristics, and how far up the incremental slope it is lodged. Much of it originates on the submerged flood plain of the Susquehanna and arrives here whenever the floodgates of the Conowingo Dam are opened.

Although the bad news is that this periodic release can result in an unsightly mess, the good news is that there's always plenty of free lumber. If I go down to scrounge through the waterlogged offerings in the aftermath of a storm, I do not come up empty-handed. As I collect, I fantasize clever recycling projects—a tool shed, a gazebo, a primitive boat on the order of a South Seas wayfaring raft. But though I've amassed a good-sized pile of wood, I haven't put any of it to more noteworthy use than as bean poles and tomato stakes.

Along the Tolchester shoreline, almost all the occupied lots are bulkheaded in one fashion or another, and between a few of them are beach indentations, signifying houseless lots or sixty-foot street-end rights-of-way. The street ends are technically owned by the Tolchester Community Association, a homeowners' organization that hosts the occasional bingo game and potluck supper, but has no funds for shoreline preservation. Most owners of empty lots, including K and me, find themselves in similar straits.

The coming quandary, against which most existing bulkheading will eventually be useless, is the rising sea level. If the industrialized nations' CO_2 emissions continue to expand at their present rate, and the greenhouse effect worsens, the bay waters will top our neighbors' and our own rip-rap in a century or two, and the shoreline will recede alarmingly (by this time, cities like Baltimore and Washington will be virtually underwater). This isn't something I actively worry about. As it is, I hardly give a thought to our unprotected bluff, which continues to crumble into the bay at a rate, on an average, of a few inches per year. Being overly concerned about the century after the next is too divagating an undertaking; one worry leads to another, and before long, the mind is plunged into neverending anxiety. It's better to sing, as I do, *que será, será.*

At the lowest tides, the beach extends forty or fifty feet from bluff base to surf; at the highest, not more than twenty feet of the beach *isn't* submerged. Taupe and somewhat coarse in texture, the predominant sand contrasts with the fine, almost spongy yellowish-brown marl that slumps into it. The bulk of the bluff itself, a variegated alluvial deposit, hearkens to an older and calmer era, when the post-Pleistocene Susquehanna was drowned as the result of glacial melting and an invasive sea. Together, the forty-foot bluff and the beach form an interface of the vertical and horizontal, a fluxional right angle in which one dimension segues into the other. The beach, smoothed by hydrodynamism, accumulates detritus, both falling and floating, which, until a surpassing tide arrives, has no place else to go. The bluff—eroded by wind and frost, rivulet-carved, and otherwise ablated by the effects of gravity—depends on the beach as its buffer zone, but cedes fractions of itself all the while.

Officious visitors, peering down along the bluff past where the rip-rap ends, make much of the beach's indentation. "What are you going to do about this?" they ask, shaking their heads as they point out the obvious. "Another twenty years, and you're not going to have a lot here anymore." Defensively, I express two considerations: first, as the bluff recedes it will be less exposed to the north, which should greatly arrest its demise; second, the sand and pebbles that are continually migrating along the bottom of the bay keep the beach from being overly subtracted from (at this writing, there actually appears to be *more* to the beach than when we first moved here). As for the rising sea level, the world body politic may get around to halting, or even reversing, the greenhouse effect. "But I'm no expert," I conclude, knowing it's better to be a rube than an arguer.

The face of the bluff, with its overhanging brush and over-dangling roots and skirt of soil, constitutes a monumental privacy screen, setting off the beach as an area unto itself. Chunk by chunk, grain by grain, the bluff's corporality slides into the sand, and the sand also shifts, and the big picture, geomorphically speaking, is one of sedimentary migration. What the beach will look like after a bad storm is anybody's guess. The bluff shows its own wear and tear from one violent episode, but not nearly so dramatically. In a day-to-day time frame, overall erosion is proceeding at a tortoise pace, although I'm sure that on a computer simulation, compressing days into centuries, the speed of the process would be nothing less than a hare's scamper.

Yet, the impetus to preserve a vacant waterfront lot isn't the same as if a structure were on it. News images of houses toppling into the sea have a way of sticking in the brain, but there's nothing but young trees and brush and grass to topple here. And none of it topples easily; roots that heretofore pushed so tenaciously into terra firma are thrust nakedly into mid-air, clinging defiantly to balls of soil, creating snags of vegetation that refuse to break off. The bluff is not going gently. Even if I could afford to protect it, I'd be loath to do so, because once rip-rapped, the beach wouldn't be around for long. Undernourished from behind and above, it would soon be under water. My wife and I are indeed fortunate to possess a beach of our very own. The last thing we want to do is obliterate it. Possession in this case means hands off; we are more than willing to concede Nature's mutability.

When I've descended the stairs and stepping stones, scrambled over the rip-rap, and set foot on the sand, none but the lustiest shout reaches me, and I hear no shout at all if the wind is blowing. Alone or with K at my side, I relish this insulation from mundane intrusions. At bay level, my perspective isn't as much an overview as it is from above, so I tend to get more thinking done. During beachwalking, abstruse concepts are mulled over, decisions arrived at. The only distraction is the water itself, stretching to a shoreline so remote it could be Atlantis, as far as my inward-seeking mind is concerned.

Lost in thought, I'm surprised by unexpected company. One of Tolchester's many dogs comes sniffing along, lifting a leg on blanched driftwood to delineate its zig-zag route. The canine has come down via a steep path to the south—paw prints tell the story, irrefutable until the tide comes in. I've seen deer tracks here, too, pressed deeply into a slumped portion of the bluff, and then they stop, as if the deer had somehow bounded uphill, back to the thicket. When I retrace my own steps on the sand, my other-directional shoe prints look forensically viable; they're so fresh that they incriminate me for walking splay-footed and having worn-down heels, not to mention less obvious shortcomings. Undoubtedly, a Sherlock Holmes could deduce all the flaws in my character from this shambling record of a gait that is anything but straight.

I spend a lot of time looking down at my feet, not glumly, but with a philosophical mien. Walking along a beach provides an opportunity to commune with the primordial self, that jot of consciousness that crept ashore tens of thousands of years ago and continues to seek solace at waterside. If antecedents of land-dwelling life forms were nurtured in such a margin as I tread upon, I can imagine how they got started. A tentative foray, a resolute will-stiffening, a venture to firmer ground, an adaptive coming to grips, and finally—as I'm doing right now—a nostalgic return journey. In so many respects, a beach is a cradle as well as a cradle's cousin, a crucible. This is the perfect place to enter into existence and forge ahead with life. The shallows of the surf host a broth of the seen and the unseen, a chowder of pecking orders, if you will. Menhaden are thriving and in turn being thrived upon, sea nettles roll with the aqueous punches. At a remove from the water, in dry sand, insects and arachnids, too, are taking care of business, and higher still, in the vertical bluff, holes an inch or two in diameter indicate habitats of additional creatures—birds? bats? snakes? rats? The beach is a veritable Copacabana. I just happen to be the only one on the scene that's drawing universal conclusions.

A breeze from the northwest enhances the depositions of a tide. When objects are washed ashore, it takes a consecutively higher flood to flush them out; even then, the flushing is usually only partially successful, for on its heels, a new crop of strandees arrives. Foremost among these is a harvest of cellulose, composed chiefly of twigs, bark, bracts, chips, slivers, slats, sticks, and stalks. Texturally interwoven, it collects in a jagged windrow that multiplies in substance as it is pushed toward the base of the bluff. Wet or dry, the cellulose has a clean appearance, for not a single iota arrives that hasn't been washed in miles and miles of water. It's odorless, lifeless, crunchy to walk on, but despite the occasionally thick accumulation, it has no bluff-preserving qualities whatsoever. It floats away, whole or in part, when the water wills it to.

But the incoming tides add much more to the beached diaspora of cellulose—an assortment that includes (but is not limited to) aerosol cans, antifreeze containers, athletic shoes, bald tires, beercans, berry boxes, blister packs, bottlecaps, broken toys, can cuffs, candy wrappers, cardboard boxes, carpentry cutoffs, Christmas decorations, condoms, crab buoys, defunct netting, drink bottles, fake fruit, fishing tackle, flowerpots, freezer boxes, laundry detergent jugs, lunchboxes, margarine tubs, meat trays, milk jugs, nose-drop dispensers, packaging pellets, paint cans, plastic pails, prescription vials, propane tanks, quart oil containers, rope, rubber thongs, safety seals, snuff cans, squeeze bottles, styrofoam cups, syringes, tampon tubes, tangled nylon line, teething rings, tennis balls, training wheels, Whiffle balls and bats, and Ziploc bags.

Even if the above catalog—minus the dead fish and crabs that were injured by humans and thrown back—sounds extensive, I do not intend it to lessen the beach's inherent aesthetic appeal. Relatively speaking, it remains a thing of beauty and a joy forever, in spite of what washes up. There is beauty, too, in the unselectivity of the tidal process. What comes, comes. If it's consumer-oriented—that is to say, if it's cheaply produced and widely distributed—chances are it floats. There's not much point in indicting the poor slobs on and about the bay who've parted with their trash, whether they did it in an appropriate manner or not, for they've been indoctrinated by an economic system that holds them in thrall to goods and goodies they believe are indispensable to their well-being. The beer (or soda or 5 percent juice-drink) *has* to be drunk; if the empty can or bottle misses the refuse barrel, or if the barrel is overflowing, or nonexistent, what's the big deal? The corporation-consumer transaction is complete—that's the principal accomplishment.

One of the most effective forms of advertising is the thrown-away package. The message is a simple one: see, everybody else can't do without it, so why should I? A discarded color-printed container is a record of individual satisfaction: *it tasted good, it quenched my thirst, it assuaged my hunger, it cured my hangover (or headache, or hemorrhoids), it kept my engine running, it got the job done, it gave me something to smile about.* Recycling is a drop in the bucket, a drop that usually boils down to a clever logo intended to deflect guilt and meet federally pipe-dreamed guidelines. Who really recycles, anyway? The fad is prehistoric by now. The bins are maxed, the converters are busted, and, worse, new generations of packaging materials don't even need the kid-gloves treatment of yore; they naturally break down in the landfills, along with the disposable diapers and the pizza crusts. Or so we're told.

No, the beach just happens to be the place where the garbage stream that misses the landfills ends up. This medley of the man-made belongs here as much as the splintery, waterlogged cellulose. It claims its rightful resting ground in plain view of *we the people*, who have elevated consumerism to something our culture cannot do without. Snazzy coloration adds piquancy to the woody browns and madders, much in the way a commercial strip on the outskirts of Anytown, U.S.A., enlivens the humdrum sideway (the competition of tall signs for reactive brain space can be downright exciting, come to think about it). The planet reverberates with appetites that have been—or have to be—acted upon. Leitmotifs of desire are worn on our collective sleeve. Concealing what has brought us to the fine fettle of the end of the second millennium is a little like putting skirts on piano legs, Victorian-style. We've got it, by golly! Why shouldn't we flaunt it?

The things we consume and dispose of, regardless of where we put them, stay in the forefront of our consciousness. Like a jingle or a catchy advertisement that gets locked in mental replay, they remind us that our well-being can be bought—and at a reasonably inexpensive price—despite the spiritual rejoinders from our sparsely attended places of worship. Yes, well-being can be bought, and so can happiness and contentment. But there is a downside: the collateral appurtenances (the stuff that doesn't get hauled away by sanitation staffers) from this easily attainable nirvana, taking into account its many variations and permutations, will never disappear from the face of the earth. Some of it is half-buried, some of it blows along the gutters and against chain-link fences, some of it is fragmented into minute particles that lodge in the liver and lungs, some of it wafts up to the ozone layer, some of it breaks down into so-called harmless muck and sludge, some of it goes into the making of other products . . . and some of it washes up on this beach.

We are nest-foulers extraordinaire; we are also dung beetles from hell. I used to believe otherwise, fervently so, but now I find it impossible to imagine planetary purity in the face of so much evidence to the contrary, rampant good intentions notwithstanding. The quart oil containers, for example, have been tossed overboard, caps rescrewed, by boaters who are too busy to stow them until the end of a cruise. Hey! it's a free country. Furthermore, there's no guilt in the tossing: no oil's gonna leak out anytime soon. Is this environmentally friendly or what?

In warm weather, when we've gone down to swim, K has been very conscientious about picking up the most glaring discards. She starts with a large container, a found object such as a market basket for crabs, or a cracked, misshapen industrial bucket, and fills it with bottles and cans and such, while I'm wordlessly criticizing the futility of her action, and only marginally assisting. (She knows what I think, but she does it anyway; it makes her feel good.) She lightens the load by banging the sand off each object: glass is tuneful, but plastic is submusical, unpercussive even. Later, I'll chivalrously haul the container over the rocks and up the steps for her. Does the beach look better for her ministrations? Of course it does, but a storm later, the coefficient of the man-made returns to its base line.

That first August, we go on vacation for two weeks and come back, road-weary, just in time for an early evening swim, only to find that trespassers have recently held a bonfire party on the sand. Their legacy leaves us feeling violated: smoldering logs, ripped six-pack cartons, smashed beer bottles. Now, broken glass is an exception I'll jump right in and help get rid of. I happen to despise it; every time I've stepped shoeless on a shard of glass, I've wished evil would befall the thoughtless jerk who left it there. Broken glass on a beach epitomizes antisocial behavior—somebody doesn't give a hoot about the welfare of the next barefoot person to come along.

The most broken glass I've ever seen on a beach was in Bermuda, of all places, about five years ago. Aching to get away from my pastel-clad fellow tourists, I walked miles to locate a people-free stretch of shoreline. I was fortunate to come across a native Bermudian who directed me to an out-of-the-way public park, down a stairway cut into coral rock, to a hidden pink jewel of a pocket beach opening onto turquoise water. It was as paradisiacal a spot as I had ever seen, and since nobody was around, I stripped off my street clothes, but didn't take two steps before realizing I was in a minefield of broken glass. *Le paradis perdu!* Gingerly, after much stooping to pick up shards in my path, I made it to the optically clear shallows, but in deeper water, I suffered a painful cut when I accidentally put my foot down. Dog sharks circling nearby only exacerbated my misery. Chastened and limping, I returned to the tourist venues.

As a result of the unauthorized bonfire party, my wife and I take two precautions: we nail up a No Trespassing sign and start wearing swim shoes. The sign, fastened to a board that's affixed to a fallen tree at the base of the bluff, infuriates a local man, who informs me that all his life he's had access to this and every other beach in Tolchester, and nobody's ever been fool enough to try to stop him. He happens to be fishing at water's edge, and I've come down to chase him away. He insists that he's within his rights, and I concede the point: legally, shorefront property extends only to the mean tidal mark. However, he's standing on dry sand, so technically he is trespassing. I feel small-minded to be splitting hairs with a neighbor, but I want to get word out that bonfire parties and beach-trashing will no longer be tolerated. Resentfully, he reels in and walks away.

Not many days later, I discover that the flimsy aluminum sign has been ripped from the board (a piece of driftwood) that held it onto the tree, crumpled, and tossed into the water. Retrieving the sign and smoothing it flat as best I can, I re-attach it to the board, using twice as many nails. The board itself has been fastened to the tree with screw-shank spikes, so it's not going anywhere. But a week later, I notice that the sign has again been pulled off and crumpled—really stomped. My efforts to flatten it out are less successful this time; nevertheless, I re-affix it to the board, riddling it with nails, not sparing the lettering, which is almost, in its present condition, indecipherable. A few more days go by and I find the sign, board and all, floating face up in the surf. Whoever did the deed must have gone down to the beach with a crowbar. I have to hand it to the perpetrator; he (or she) is more persistent than I figured him (or her) to be. Bowing to local custom, I decide to leave the sign down. After fishing it out of the water, I fling it onto the bluff base, where it lies to this day, upside-down, offending nobody, proclaiming its message to ants and millipedes and worms.

As for the swim shoes, they take a little getting used to. They remind me of the rubbers my mother insisted I wear over my shoes on rainy days back in elementary school. A shod swim isn't quite so free and easy at first, but I make the adjustment. Swimming in the bay is delightfully different from swimming in the ocean. The water isn't as salty, the waves aren't as high. Also, there's no undertow to speak of, except when a deep-draft vessel goes by. Sometimes, in a neap tide, a ship's wave will hit the beach and generate a back-wave, a roller in reverse. These are scarier to watch than to be caught in, but a few years ago off the Tolchester marina, where the shipping channel passes at its closest, a young child playing on a jetty was swept away in a back-wave and drowned. The incident prompted the Maryland Pilots Association to lower channel speed limits, which at present appear to be largely adhered to.

It's easy to see why the beach is the recipient of all excesses and errors. Temporary discoloration of the sand can indicate a minor unreported oil spill, the residue of which clings to my beard when I emerge from a swim. In the water, I can't see or smell it, but coagulated brown scum rubs off on the towel. Whatever leaky fuel barge or tanker is responsible, nobody will ever know; it's not easy to finger an incrementally polluting culprit. Given the quantity of shipping that goes past in proportion to the severity of the spill, I should be happy. Things could be worse, a lot worse—just ask the folks on Prince William Sound.

The beach is thus a prime indicator, a detection strip. The hydrocarbons, the storm trash, the eroding bluff, the American way of life—it's all a read-out, a bellwether of the regional, if not global environment. What is found on the sand illustrates the fact that hindsight has more clarity than foresight and actions always speak louder than words. No further proofs are necessary to illustrate the feverish pitch with which we bequeath to future generations the excesses of our own. It's not enough to fall back on the old that's-the-way-it-is-and-we-can't-do-much-about-it excuse, nor is it acceptable to offer the hoary pretext that God told us to be fruitful and multiply.

As a relative newcomer, I haven't witnessed the long-term degradation of Chesapeake Bay, but I've kept tabs, more or less, on a parallel situation in Rhode Island's Narragansett Bay. Having grown up near there in the 1950s, I have distinct memories of how the beaches looked. I remember rubbery ruffles of seaweed and honest-to-goodness driftwood: slats from lobster pots, planking from wrecked boats. Everything that washed up *belonged* to the sea—and ultimately was returned. In my earliest impressions, the Rhode Island beaches weren't clean in the sense of having been cleaned, although the hurricane of 1938 had done some high-powered scouring that was still talked about by old-timers. The sand, elementally holystoned, had a taken-for-granted purity. Although the beaches weren't exactly unspoiled— what beach can be considered unspoiled after the first print of a human foot?—they were, by today's canon, pollution-free.

Ten years later, vacationing in those familiar haunts, I became aware for the first time of the widespread presence of human-generated trash. Things lay drying on the sand that didn't belong to the sea, but I remember being more amused than concerned. Beachcombing was becoming an altogether novel kind of treasure hunt. To heck with shells! I picked up popsicle sticks, nuggets of weatherbeaten glass, chunks of cork and kapok, orphaned plastic shovels, milk-bottle caps, triangularly punctured cans of Rheingold and Ballantine. Gradually, a broader range of offal washed up, too, from the offshore garbage dumping that was growing in proportion to the shipping and fishing industries.

Still, it was only a smattering compared to what I would find ten years after that, when the Rhode Island coastline seemed trashed beyond redemption. Waterwashed junk was crammed between the revetment boulders off Point Judith, and seaweed had slipped to a distant second place vis-à-vis beach litter. It seemed that the entire seashore had succumbed to that sorry end-product of consumerism: the empties. Viewing the evidence from my emerging artistic standpoint, I was inspired to do a photographic essay. The cast-offs had a certain manqué appeal; they seemed to mock human self-importance. In their shapes, broken or whole, they reflected the engines of civilization, but now, having fulfilled the role of wrapper-container-advertiser-in-one, they were amassed in a random mix, a collage of disconected images. Perfectly exhibited they were, too—shadowed, wetted, nestled, evermore useless, form bereft of function. Clicking my camera, I leapt from rock to rock and splashed along the surf in pursuit of my scoop. Whether or not my results were published (as it turned out, they weren't), I felt I was contributing to a valid twentieth-century archive. I was documenting Nature's entrapment of the artificial.

This integration of the manufactured with the natural, as I see it today on Chesapeake Bay, has prompted me to relax my standards with respect to what is bemoaned as no longer *pristine*. There is no such word in the lexicon anymore. No body of air or water or land exists without the scars of human intervention, which, even if it can't be perceived by the senses, can still be measured by instruments. Today, the only things we can truly call pristine are consumer items in their original packaging—and a better term for pristine, in this instance, is *brand new*. In our pell-mell rush to expand and conquer, we can't even enter the virgin territory of the cosmos without leaving our mark of Cain. Space junk orbits high above Earth like a tinny halo. Exhaust trails us wherever we go. Wimps are just as culpable as bruisers. Society expects us to be both mature and youthful at the same time, and that is perhaps the worst way to be, since it allows us to temper our culpability with innocence. We know we're befouling the bay, but we're having such a damn good time, why spoil the fun?

I'm beginning to see that the world is headed toward a new paradigm in which Nature encompasses an acceptable threshold of human-generated trash. Again, this beach is a prime example: no matter how assiduously K cleans up one small area, it returns to littered normalcy after a tide or two. I hardly think of the beach as being polluted anymore—*stuff washes up*, that's all. If we had a couple of refuse barrels down there, like the ones on a municipal strand, we could do our daily good deed, but why bother when the next nor'easter will take care of it for us?

In the new paradigm, idealism bows to reality, recognizing that population pressure and its attendant ramifications are here to stay. Nature struggles along, just like everybody else. With trash in her matrix, she is prouder than ever and all the more precious to behold. The beach is no less a beach for all that washes up—I need to believe this as a credo; I cannot allow myself to be dismayed. The foibles of humanity are spread out on the sand, a study in contrast to the tough old bird that Nature herself still is. The waves keep pounding, the bluff keeps crumbling. Nibbling or roaring, the bay has to accommodate all the insults and injuries that will continue for careless years to come. I take it on faith that the surf remains synonymous with a heartbeat, compelling a respiration that is not about to surrender its last breath anytime soon.

chapter
4

At Chesapeake City, a forty-minute drive to the north, on a chilly Thursday evening in February, I meld into what, for this size town, is an unusually large crowd. USCGC *Red Birch* (WLM 687), the buoytender I've been watching on and off for months now, is moored for a one-night open house. Curiosity has gotten the better of me, as apparently it has for many others; before the evening is over, some six hundred will have come aboard.

Lt. Donald E. Jaccard, *Red Birch*'s commanding officer, a Cecil County native, is something of a local hero, having graduated from Bohemia Manor High School in 1978 and joined the Coast Guard, coming up through the ranks as an enlisted man. I spot him in a throng of admirers; he's compactly built, rosy-cheeked and boyish in his blue working uniform. Indeed, all crew members appear youthful and up to their ears in visitor management.

When I introduce myself as a writer, Lt. Jaccard offers me a personal tour. He starts off with a quick rundown of the ship's history. *Red Birch* was commissioned in 1965, the third of five 157-foot coastal buoytenders constructed in the Coast Guard Yard at Curtis Bay, MD, where she is currently homeported. Displacing 525 tons, with a draft of six feet seven inches, she is well suited to the shallow estuaries and tributaries of Chesapeake Bay, although her first eleven years of service were in San Francisco Bay. Back in the Baltimore area since 1976, *Red Birch* also serves as an icebreaker, having a reinforced prow and powerful enough main engines (two 900-horsepower D398 Caterpillar diesels) to push through two feet of pack ice. The cutter's most noteworthy characteristic is her maneuverability. With her twin controllable pitch propellers, bow thruster, and electro-hydraulic hand tiller—instead of a ship's wheel—she can be turned on the proverbial dime.

Red Birch has accommodations for six officers, two chief petty officers, and thirty enlisted crew members. The ship's primary mission is Aids to Navigation, which involves maintaining 387 buoys marking the major shipping channels in Chesapeake Bay from Alexandria, Virginia, and the Potomac River, northward to Baltimore and just beyond Pooles Island. This constitutes more buoys to service than any other Coast Guard tender, and the crew's pride is reflected in the ship's motto: *America's hardest working buoytender.* Between April and November, in addition to scheduled buoy maintenance, the cutter is engaged for several weeks restoring various lighthouses around the bay.

At length, Lt. Jaccard makes a suggestion that I've been too modest to pursue: would I be interested in joining *Red Birch* for a day's sail to see firsthand what buoytending is all about? *Would I?!* Three weeks later, at 0630 hours, I'm turning onto the entrance road to the U.S. Coast Guard Yard at Curtis Bay, the last exit off I-695 eastbound before the Key Bridge, and brandishing my driver's license to the sentry on duty. I've never been in the Coast Guard Yard; it's at least an hour before the first civilian work shift and slightly spooky. The aisles of anonymous cavernous buildings bring to mind the exterior of a movie studio. Arriving pierside, I come upon a truly bizarre sight: several bargeloads of buoys blinking like crazy in the waning darkness. More blinking buoys are lying on their sides around the parking lot. Lighted buoys up close and out of the water are big, some twenty feet in length from lens to counterweight. Except for their size, electrification, and enhanced radar visibility, modern buoys haven't evolved much beyond their predecessors; basically, they're watertight steel cans with lifting bails and padeyes welded to them so that they can be (1) anchored to the bottom they're supposed to warn about, and (2) taken out of service when necessary.

In the three most heavily trafficked channels where *Red Birch*

operates—the Brewerton Eastern Extension that leads into the
bay from Baltimore and the Patapsco River, the Craighill Channel running to the southern bay, and the Upper Chesapeake Bay
Channel (the one off our bluff) that is the deep-draft route to the
C&D Canal—there are sixty-seven lighted buoys that need to be
changed seasonally. These buoys come in two types (along with
two colors, red and green): a 12,000-pound regular buoy and a
5,000-pound ice buoy. The regular buoy, which is in service from,
roughly, March 15 to December 15, has a cylindrical "two-pocket
integrity" hull, counterweighted with a downward shaft, and a
tower rising above that supports the lighting apparatus. The ice
buoy, in service a scant three months, tapers conically both
above and below the waterline, a shape that lets it ride out the
abrasion and submersion caused by moving ice. Since a regular
buoy stays "on watch" twice as long as an ice buoy, it is powered
by one to six deep-cycle batteries rechargeable by solar panel.
The panel, from seventeen to twenty-four inches square, is flat-
mounted directly above the lens on four aluminum rods and
capped with a clear Lexan pyramid that is guano-proof (birds love
to sit on the buoys, but rain does the housecleaning). Ice buoys
are powered by primary batteries only, the equivalent of several
hundred D-cells in a long narrow pack inserted behind a watertight lens dome. Primary battery life is a maximum of 120 days.

All lighted buoys are differentiated by their pulse, or the intervals of their flash at night, distinctions that are marked on
navigation charts. A regular buoy will flash brighter than an ice
buoy because its 0.55- to 1.15-ampere light is contained in a
taller lens. Not long after dawn, a photoelectric diode breaks the
power circuit of both types, so the batteries stop draining, and, in
a regular buoy, actually recharge. By day, a regular buoy is also
more visible than an ice buoy because of its profile: the vertically sided hull—originally designed to hold the acetylene tanks
of earlier light systems—and partially open framework tower.
The tower not only supports the lens and solar array, but also a
snorkel-type vent pipe for the batteries (ice buoy batteries, like
those of a flashlight, do not need to be vented).

Although the hull of an ice buoy is unitary and accessible only through the lens dome, the hull of a regular buoy has two bolt-down watertight hatches, one for each battery compartment. It is not uncommon, however, to see a quick-fix battery box mounted on the tower when a battery has died between regular servicing intervals, since work within a hatch is best done when the buoy is out of the water. The light mechanism itself is more failsafe; the lamp changer, a hexagonal holder with six mounted bulbs, automatically ratchets a fresh bulb into the circuit when the filament of the old bulb breaks. Short of being hit by a ship and sunk—which occasionally happens, although it is never reported by the perpetrator, but by the next vessel that comes along—all lighted buoys are reasonably trouble-free. Their visibility at night is their raison d'être. When an oceangoing merchant ship, its navigation bridge eighty feet above the water, sluices along a channel after dark, bell or gong "cans" and "nuns" simply aren't noticeable enough.

Two other items grab my attention now that I'm pierside to *Red Birch*, across from the blinking reds and greens. The first is a neatly stacked mountain of cast concrete blocks; in the pre-dawn light, it could be mistaken for the start of a Giza pyramid. Each block is eight feet square and five feet tall and is technically known as a sinker. Weighing 18,000 pounds, with a six-inch lifting bail embedded in its top center, one sinker anchors one buoy to the bottom of the bay. In place and "mudded in," a sinker would appear to be immovable, and so it is under most circumstances. Still, sinkers can be dragged by errant ships as well as by ice, causing—in Coast Guard parlance—"buoy discrepancies."

The second attention-grabber is the heavy steel chain that lies in impressive heaps and piles, each link an inch and a quarter to an inch and a half in diameter. I can't begin to imagine what a shot (a ninety-foot unit of chain measurement) must weigh. Links of this beefiness, and as plainly forged, have an anachronistic look: they could have been stretched across the Baltimore harbor entrance to keep out British men-of-war in 1813. Some of the chain appears new, orange with rain rust; some is abraded, some is barnacle encrusted. A buoy is tethered to a sinker by a short two-shackle bridle of chain with a ring in its mid-point, from which the main portion of the anchoring chain hangs down in a loose arc like the letter L with a curve instead of a ninety-degree angle. In twenty feet of water, there will be seventy-five feet of chain, creating what is termed a *watch circle* in which the sinker is placed precisely in the center, and the buoy drifts within the circle as far as the chain allows. The curved L of chain has three sections: the horizontal portion coming from the sinker and lying in the mud is called the *bottom*; the section that curves toward the vertical and takes the abrasion of the buoy swings is called the *chafe*; the vertical section joined to the buoy is called the *riser*. A buoy can thus be hoisted aboard a tender, along with two-thirds of its chain length, without disturbing the sinker. Chafe sections out of the water are routinely inspected by micrometer, measured for wear to thirty-seconds of an inch, and replaced, if necessary, by cutting out the old section with an oxyacetylene torch and shackling in a new approximately twenty-five-foot length.

Making sure I'm well bundled up, including hat (my old Navy watchcap), scarf, and gloves, I cross the cutter's brow for the second time. I'm met by Lt. (jg) Kathryn Dunbar, the executive officer and only woman aboard. She ushers me into the officers' wardroom, where I find Lt. Jaccard seated at the head of the table, finishing a bowl of raisin bran. Warmly welcomed, I'm invited to join in breakfast, and even though I ate just an hour earlier, I don't turn it down.

A coffee mug later, I follow Lt. Jaccard up two ladders to the navigation bridge, where the duty watch is readying the ship for getting underway. I am already familiar with the bridge from my earlier visit—its black rubber-matted floor, CO's chair, chart desk, twelve-inch chrome hand tiller, compass, variable-pitch controls, bow thruster lever, radar repeaters, bridge-to-bridge radio, depth finder, ECPINS—acronym for Electronic Chart Positioning Integrated Navigation System—screens, and personnel-specific binoculars. There's excellent visibility from the shaded bank of windows fore and aft, several of which crank down. At either side of the bridge is a hinged weather-tight door that leads to a blue-canopied wing, port and starboard. Each wing is provided with repeating propulsion and steering controls, as well as an alidade for shooting bearings.

State-of-the-art technology plays a major role in the functioning of the buoytender. DGPS (Differential Global Positioning System) navigation—the same digitally enhanced geosynchronous orbiting system that tells a pilot where a plane is, or a hiker where he or she is located in the woods—provides an instantly graspable readout of the ship's location. On the two ECPINS screens, *Red Birch* is a blinking target, always central in a changing map of the surroundings (at present, I'm studying the contours of the bulkheading at the Coast Guard Yard). The ECPINS readout, in combination with a conventional nautical chart, is an embarrassment of riches: it's hard to tell which is a backup of which, so bountiful—and accurate—are the details. Redundant systems, including four pairs of eyes (the deck watch officer, the quartermaster of the watch, the helmsman, and the lookout), plus radarscopy and the paper and electronic charts, ensure that the ship isn't going anywhere it isn't supposed to.

A further refinement of DGPS technology, called LAAPS (Laptop Automated Aid Positioning System), developed by the Coast Guard and in use on *Red Birch* since 1992, is displayed on two smaller black-and-white screens: crosshairs that show exactly where a buoy belongs within a yard or two. This program is run via a portable computer on the chart desk and is so precise that it keys in the *offset* from the DGPS antenna on the mainmast to the chain stopper on the buoy deck, the point from which a sinker plunges straight to the bottom. Positioning the easily maneuverable tender, its chain stopper represented by a small dot or "bug" on the screen, to the crosshairs until the command "Shackle and hang!" is called out by the control-jiggling deck watch officer, assures buoy placement with negligible error.

Yet for all its newfangled gear, *Red Birch* is slated to be decommissioned soon. A thirty-three-year-old cutter can be retrofitted cost-effectively only so many times. The next generation of buoytenders will incorporate all these new technologies and more, including a computer-driven control known as DPS (Dynamic Positioning System), an integration of ECPINS and LAAPS that will hold the ship over a buoy position without hands-on effort. Also, the new Coast Guard tenders will be one hundred seventy-five feet long, eighteen feet longer than *Red Birch*, and they'll be crewed by eighteen persons, fewer than half the present complement. This cutback of sailor power is hard to conceptualize as we get underway, when everybody on the entire ship except me appears to be actively engaged. Down on the buoy deck, a crew is making last-minute checks of the three regular buoys, chocked and secured, which will be replacing three ice buoys. One of the buoys will get the new sinker, too, sitting like a pillbox on the deck centerline.

As dawn breaks, *Red Birch* slips beneath I-695 and the Pennington Avenue drawbridge, which has been opened. In ten minutes, we've left Curtis Bay, turning onto the Brewerton Channel, where two dredges, *Super Scoop* and *Virginian*, are transferring clamshellsful of bottom silt to awaiting barges. Apart from the dredges, there's no river traffic to speak of. One tug passes, pushing a small but lethal cargo of sulphuric acid. On the banks are trios and quartets of smokestacks with emission plumes, but the industrial landscape is monotonous enough not to be accorded more than passing interest: you've seen one chemical factory, you've seen them all. I'm more captivated by the professionalism of the bridge personnel and the bright graphics of the nearest ECPINS screen with its minutely advancing moving target (us). In gunmetal tones, the day materializes.

The captain is pointing out details of some of the buoys we pass. One has a list that may be evidence of a slow leak (before buoys are deployed, their hulls are pressure-tested to three pounds per square inch). Another buoy has a scabbed-on battery box midway up its tower (collisions, even slight ones, can knock out lamp electrics). Another buoy has a bent, though still functioning, solar array—a cocked hat. The captain tells of a buoy that was reported missing recently, most likely sunk by an off-course deep-draft ship or a tug with a crabbed tow. With the aid of a bottom scanner, the buoy was successfully grappled, repaired on deck, and put back on watch.

As I listen to him speak, I begin to realize the care that accompanies the execution of the ship's primary mission. Each of the 387 buoys in *Red Birch*'s purview is described and updated on an Aid Positioning Record, a sheet the captain personally fills out and later files on computer. He shows me the sheet for lighted buoy #8 on the Brewerton Eastern Extension—it'll be the first buoy we'll work on today, and we're almost there—on which is notated its precise position: North 39 degrees, 09 minutes, 59.856 seconds; West 76 degrees, 23 minutes, 30.318 seconds. Before DGPS, buoy location was ascertained by shooting horizontal sextant angles, triangulating with landmarks such as watertowers and smokestacks. Buoy #8 has a watch circle radius of 24 feet, and a chain length of 23.86 yards. Other facts pertaining to the buoy include the last time it was painted, its battery and lamp service record, and the latest micrometric measure of its chafe section. The sheet also notes that the present ice buoy is held in place by two 8,500-pound sinkers. The single 18,000-pounder we're carrying on deck will be their replacement.

The wind chill is devastating on the bridge wing where Ens. Russell Bowman, the duty watch officer, is at the controls, drawing *Red Birch* alongside the ice buoy that's about to be relieved. He's in his Mustang, an insulated wind- and water-resistant coverall, with a generously earflapped hat and catalytic warmers in his mittens, and still he's cold. One deck below, behind glass, is the boom operator, who's following the hand signals of the buoy deck supervisor down among the hard-hatted deck crew. In addition, there's a safety supervisor standing on the fo'c'sle.

On the forestay between mainmast and mizzenmast, just forward of the stack, have been hoisted "day shapes," the black canvas ball-diamond-ball arrangement that signifies that the cutter is restricted in maneuverability. Channel traffic will have to go around *Red Birch*. The chain restraint across the buoy port is withdrawn, the crane boom swings up and away from its mooring. The boom has two lift points, the "whip" on its tip, and the "main" eight feet back, which can lift 8,000 and 20,000 pounds, respectively. Ens. Bowman has the ship's hull almost against the buoy, close enough to gaff a lifting bail. A line is secured, next the "whip" hook; then, in strict procedure with permissions sought and granted between fo'c'sle and bridge, the ice buoy is raised out of the water. With the aid of lanyards, the dripping buoy is maneuvered directly above the chain stopper, where a link in its riser is entrapped and hammered home by a deckhand wielding a sledge hammer, thus relieving the tension on the buoy itself, which is lowered onto the deck, then unshackled.

At the controls, dancing to keep warm, Ens. Bowman is maintaining "up and down," that is, keeping the stoppered chain vertical. He's constantly referring to the computer screen behind the side window. By aligning the "bug" with the crosshairs, he's got the cutter right where he wants it. The engine revolutions hold a constant 900 rpm as he alters the propellers' pitch from forward to reverse, working tiller and bow thruster as well. The "main" hook swings down and hoists up another section of chain, which is locked anew in the stopper. The chafe is easily recognizable, twenty feet or so of rust-free gray: color-wise, it looks new, but thickness-wise, it'll probably have to be cut out and replaced.

In the next lift, the two 8,500-pound mud-covered sinkers break the surface of the water, but before they're hoisted aboard, a crewmember hoses them down. They look puny compared with the monolithic sinker that will replace them; they're stowed and disconnected. Meanwhile, a deck seaman is already busy with the oxyacetylene torch, cutting out the worn chafe. Twenty-four feet of inch-and-a-half links will replace the worn inch-and-a-quarter section, and they'll be shackled in by the time-tested "heat and beat" method—shackle pins inserted, heated red hot, and hammered till their ends are deformed enough to hold fast. There's no surer way to put chain back together. Another word for it is *blacksmithing*.

The "main" cable drums groan as the boom winches up the 18,000-pound sinker; it is left hanging over the side, secured in the chain stopper, causing a noticeable list to the ship. Next, the regular buoy is attached to both "whip" and "main" and carried vertically to the edge of the deck. After a last-minute integrity check, it is picked up by the "main" hook and left hanging at an angle just over the side, barely in the water. The approximately seventy-eight feet of chain between buoy and sinker are festooned on deck—lightly tied with rottenstop to the bull-chain, six feet of heavy deck-fastened linkage that will help control the rapid paying out of the buoy chain when the stopper is tripped. Chain is always manipulated with crooked rods called *chain hooks*. Deck seamen have been trained never to touch "live" chain with their hands, and to never, ever step between it and the water.

The chain stopper—*Red Birch* has two, one port and one starboard, welded to the gunwale plating forward in the buoy ports—is the critical component of any sinker- and buoy-setting operation. It's a nineteenth-century device, a hinged wedge held nearly vertical by a latching mechanism with a pin inserted for safety. In the wedge is one link of chain, going nowhere. When the pin is removed, the latch is struck with a sledgehammer blow so that it flies off the wedge, which flips down and instantly releases the chain. It's a simple mechanical procedure, but because of the great masses and weights involved, and the speed with which the chain rattles downward, it can be a dangerous moment unless everything is exactly right. Moreover, the chain stopper has to be precisely over its target so that the sinker can be dropped with a negligible margin of error.

Permission to "shackle and hang" is requested when each phase of the buoy deck operation has been double-checked. Then, if the "bug" is still aligned with the crosshairs, the duty watch officer calls out the command, the chainstopper is tripped, and the writhing links make a sound like bricks toppling across the deck. Sinker and chain, or chain alone, splash into the drink, and, if all goes well, the buoy is lowered the last few feet, unhooked, its lanyard released. As *Red Birch* moves away, the buoy creates a series of small concentric waves from the sudden new weight and constraint of its chain—a curtsy, as it were, announcing the commencement of its solitary watch.

After lunch, I talk with Lt. (jg) Dunbar as she works the bridge wing controls (she's duty watch officer now) on buoy #24. She's slender, almost skinny, in her late twenties, tersely efficient in both manner and speech. Her maintaining "up and down" is different from Ens. Bowman's; where he used plenty of body English, she prefers straightforward digital manipulation, and her results are just as impressive. I ask her the obvious question: what's it like to be a woman in the midst of thirty-seven men? She says she doesn't give it much thought. I ask if she's the first woman to serve on *Red Birch*, and she replies that she's the fourth. All have been XOs, or executive officers, she adds, because of the lack of separate accommodations. Aha! now I understand: her cabin, across the companionway from the captain's, is the only other space on board with a private toilet and shower. In other words, she was billeted because of bathroom availability. Suddenly, I comprehend one other reason for retiring the aging 157s: they were built for male crews only. As if reading my thoughts, Dunbar informs me that the new 175s will have gender-balanced crew accommodations. Will she stay in the Service long enough to see duty on one of the new cutters, I ask. She laughs. If things go right with her career, she says, she'll pull desk duty on her next tour, rise an increment in rank, and then be *captain* of a 175.

The day goes pretty much as expected, the sun stays out, one more buoy (#28) gets changed, and when we turn to head back toward Curtis Bay, we've gone just far enough north to glimpse the swelling of Mitchell's Bluff and the green-roofed house behind its wintry barricade of trees. By 3 P.M. we're cruising along the return leg of the Brewerton Eastern Extension, and the closer we get to Baltimore, the more channel traffic we encounter. Tugs and deep-drafts are coming in our direction, even as we overtake slower tows and meandering workboats. Bridge-to-bridge radio is the key to collision avoidance. Identifying itself, each vessel relays information and intention well ahead of crunch time, and if the passing is going to be close, both parties double-check their plans and do not waver. The radio communication is spare and cordial, but to the point. Amazingly, ships can glide within yards of one another in perfect safety.

On this return voyage, Q.M.1 Mark Sheaffer is in charge of the bridge, all line officers having retired below, and he's doing a splendid job, but rounding a bend in the Patapsco where the traffic is particularly heavy, he's dutybound to call the captain back to the bridge. Lt. Jaccard arrives just as a car carrier is hoving around a turn directly behind an empty ore freighter that's bearing down on us, and we're coming abreast of a slow tug, with barge, that's not keeping as far to the right as it could. On radio, everybody's worked out a plan, but it's too close for comfort. The barge inches to starboard as *Red Birch* passes—according to the rules of the road, the overtaking vessel bears the onus of responsibility for avoiding collision—while at the same time, the towering scarred bow of the ore freighter slips past our port beam, near enough for me to scrutinize its weld seams. Throughout these tense moments, the captain hasn't said a word, but his presence on the bridge communicates an unspoken authority. Later, after the car carrier has passed and the channel vista opens up a bit, he quietly says, "Good job, Sheaffer," and the petty officer responds with an "Aye, Sir," not taking his eyes off the water ahead.

Turning into Curtis Bay, we pass a Washington, D.C., city fireboat, the *John H. Glenn, Jr.,* which somewhat testily informs us by radio that a couple of buoys aren't where the charts say they're supposed to be. The fireboat is obviously unfamiliar with this channel. What is it doing in Baltimore, anyway? According to Lt. Jaccard's experienced eye, every buoy in the vicinity is correctly on watch. Still, he instructs Q.M.1 Sheaffer to be unfailingly polite. Sheaffer presses the mike button: "John Glenn, this is Red Birch. We hear what you're saying and will look into the matter. Thanks for bringing it to our attention." Back comes the self-important reply, "This is the John *H.* Glenn, *Jr.* I trust you'll fix the problem soon, over and out." The captain asks Sheaffer to send one final message, bidding the fireboat a pleasant afternoon.

Almost home, we're heading toward another snafu: it seems that nobody's on duty to open the Pennington Avenue bridge, which we'll reach in about five minutes. Sheaffer radios repeatedly, but the drawbridge operator has either stepped out or is asleep at the switch. It takes a cellular telephone call to the central bridge tender authority to request that the span be opened. Lt. Jaccard says it's not the first time there have been delays here, and he recounts a funny story about a drawbridge operator in Louisiana who insisted that her clearance was five feet more than it actually was. Belatedly, just as Q.M.1 Sheaffer is getting ready to cut engine speed, the bridge halves start to move upward.

In another few minutes, we're back at the Coast Guard Yard, nudging the pier and slipping our mooring lines over the bollards. I know a lot more about buoys than I did ten hours ago, and I've made a number of new friends. To cement my new bond to *Red Birch*, the captain promises he'll put my name on the list for the upcoming decommissioning ceremony. After good-byes and handshakes all around, I cross the brow and walk to the car. My sea legs feel a little strange on the solidity of asphalt, and my inner ear is still convinced that I'm gently pitching and yawing on the well-marked thoroughfares of the bay.

chapter
5

A stickler for scientific exactitude will insist that wind doesn't blow; rather, it is sucked. Empirical experience at the edge of the bay, however, confirms that it blows. And blows and blows. Wind is the constant that spans the seasons, the atmospheric equivalent of background interference—a sound and a pressure to be lived with all, or nearly all, of the time.

The wind here has no name. It comes from across the water, typically from the northwest, and varies in magnitude, from barely shimmering the grass to overturning the lawn furniture. It can be characterized as the force against which all things dare to stand. Nothing escapes it, nothing dodges out of its way. The imprint of its presence is everywhere, and when it dies down, there's almost a preternatural calm, a void where there was a dimension.

Wind that bludgeons the bleak bluff crest in winter, wind that floats the fragrance of honeysuckle in spring, wind that staves off the swamp-bred mosquitoes in summer and, in fall, launches the leaves out of the trees. Wind that caresses, wind that clouts, wind that rustles, wind that howls. Zephyrs that cool the hammock-slumberer in an otherwise stifling shade. Breezes that ruffle the wild onion and foxtail. Gusts that factor into the brains of seagulls as they wheel overhead; that gradually reduce the flag on the flagpole to tatters; that shake the steel bulkhead door leading to the cellar (and actually fling it open once in a while); that infiltrate weathersealing, rattle storm sashes, pry up the shingles.

Out on the bay, wind works visual magic. Areas affected by

surface turbulence appear darker, like long shifting bars reconfiguring and disappearing before the eyes. Wind's kinetic effect is
the best reason I know to live in a house beside water; before
coming here, I used to build ponds for the sole purpose of looking
at them and watching the wind's workings. My agrarian neighbors often misunderstood me on this point. While they fished,
gigged frogs, and watered livestock, I just stood on the bank con-
templating mirages of information. Now, before an infinitely
larger body of water, I watch the wind's sleight-of-hand and have
trouble tearing myself away. In every nuance and current, from
close-up to miles distant, something of consequence is going on.
When the wind picks up, the water begins to dance, from minuet
to saraband to waltz, and when the blow is sustained, it's a polka
of whitecaps egged on by a harsh harmonic orchestra. Billowing
sails are testament, and so is the sour tang of ships' stacks. Luck-
ily, the duration of the dance never wearies the dancer.

At its most ferocious, the wind cracks living boughs and tilts
tree trunks already teetering on the edge of the bluff, exposing
a lacework of roots. Forty feet below, waves berate the rip-rap,
flinging spray like saliva, spray that shines or glazes the boulders, depending on the temperature. January winds that blast for
days freeze the bay itself into a rough white terrain that cracks
and sings with tidal and navigational stress. Along the wintry
beach, the wave's reach turns into something akin to frozen
baclava: brittle, paper-thin sheets that crunch softly when
stepped on.

No two consecutive days in any season pass without, as my
dictionary puts it, "a natural movement of air of any velocity;
esp: air in natural motion horizontally." Across the open water,
this wind meets no impediment until it hits the bluff face, creating the updraft that blows through here with a sustained low
whistle. There's cleansing, preemptive joy in standing (or walking) exposed to it as long as the wind-chill can be tolerated;
otherwise, it's pure agony. Hair is tousled, eyes water, skin red-
dens, but the overall effect leads to self-awareness, for when the
wind is blowing hard, the cobwebs "upstairs" can also be torn

asunder. Sometimes my mental doldrums need exactly this kind of a shove. Call it a broom, call it free therapy—there's constructive meaning in the phrase "casting words upon the wind." I do it all the time, and although another term for it is talking to myself, I know I'm deriving significant benefit therefrom.

In the years I was growing up inland, steady wind seemed to exist only in the abstract: the friction of air molecules against the vehicular skin of some man-made object hurtling its way into the *Guinness Book of Records*—the thing that gave Chuck Yeager his bumpy ride in the Bell X-1, the thing that wiped out the challengers at Bonneville Flats. Wind, like time, was a medium to streak through and overcome. Aerodynamic design was the solution; if the nose (cone) and the leading and trailing edges were shaped right, mission success would follow. Rockets, fighter jets, bullet trains, Indy 500 cars—these also made wind of their own. The relativity of speed, that prodigal offspring of the twentieth century, minimized the impact and usefulness of any natural breeze. Windmills were dismantled, clotheslines gave way to clothes dryers, open windows to air-conditioners. The only wind people talked about was metaphorical: winds of war, winds of change, and then, of course, the subway-grating whoosh that lifted Marilyn Monroe's white dress.

Small wonder the scientific litany began about wind being sucked. But nowadays, with our heightened awareness of pop meteorology via the television newsroom, wind is perceived as a temporary discombobulation. At its worst, it is an inconvenience—a horizontally blown blizzard, a wiper-defying downpour. The surprise factor of hurricanes and tornadoes and typhoons has all but disappeared. Forewarning is honed to a fine art; commercial-blitzed viewers are habitually encouraged to stay tuned for the next brought-to-you-by report. The name pool for tropical storms keeps expanding. Folksy rapid-fire banter between talking heads strongly recommends prudence on the part of the affected citizen. If it's a gale-force wind, and you're on the road, your best bet is to drop back to the speed limit.

The subtext of all this—assuming you've safely reached your

destination—is *stay indoors, stay out of the weather*. I make a point of doing just the opposite. When the wind blows hard, I prefer to be out in it. From the vantage of Mitchell's Bluff, wind is *the* consummate force—a rival of gravity, a handmaiden of the tides. Wind is the thing that injects sparkle and whips up fury. At its whim is the tenor of the bay, sculpted in never-ending transformation. If I were to miss all this, I would truly be just marking time.

Feeling the breeze in my face, I ruminate on a favorite topic: self-sufficiency. There's energy blowing by me that's completely going to waste. The chapter on humanity's use of wind, though now largely unread, has yet to be fully written. Everybody knows the sheer profligacy of windpower, how it is poised to be tapped by existing technology, if it can ever be wedded to sizeable capital investment. At the moment, there are no takers, no visionaries, not even me (all my fine talk is wind of another kind—hot air). Meanwhile, across the Bay, coal-fired generating stations continue as before: the coal produces steam, the turbines spin, the transmission lines hum, and the tall smokestacks belch.

But is it not obvious that wind, the great purifier, *is* very much at work, perhaps more now than at any other time in human history? In volume alone, wind-processed air is cleansed of particulate matter to parts per billion or even trillion as it rushes eastward over the planetary surface. Wind carries away the fumes of cities, the smoke of forest fires, the water vapor from floods, the radiation from nuclear accidents. Stagnant air, wind's opposite, kills by suffocation where ozone and other pollutants gain the upper hand. The wind's regenerative abilities are neither well documented nor widely appreciated, but no single system of pollution abatement works as efficiently, or as cheaply. Yes, the wind continues to blow for free, and for that reason, the biosphere remains as nurturing to life as it has ever been.

My earliest interactions with wind have cast indelible memories. When I was six, my sister, just turned eight, was given a full-size step-through bicycle for her birthday. As she learned to ride it, so, with her permission, did I, although I was too small to reach the pedals from a seated position. Standing on them and wobbling precipitously, I managed to walk cyclically above the ground. Straightaways were my forte, where I could concentrate on balance instead of steering.

But one time, I got out on a level road in a headwind and was literally blown to a stop. I just didn't weigh enough to keep the pedals in motion. Vexed, I turned the bike around and aimed for home, and on this return leg, my cresting and dipping profile acted as a sail. How I sped! Unfortunately, neither my steering nor braking skills were up to the velocity I was attaining, and I crashed in the front yard, scraping up those brand-new fenders, not to mention my shins, and spoiling my chances of ever borrowing the bike again.

I also flew kites. They cost twenty-five cents at the corner store—eight or ten were always stowed, tightly rolled, in an umbrella stand next to the candy shelves. Aside from the coloration of the tissue paper, I'd never know what I was buying, graphics-wise, until I got home. A tiger? A starburst? A saberjet? Assembly was always a treat: inserting the tissue paper's exposed string points into notched crossbars (two thin spars of spruce fastened with a loose metal staple), tensioning the horizontal bar convexly, tying the bridle at the black printed dots. Such constructive moments were always coupled with fervent wishes for a strong wind, which could never be counted on.

Purchasing a ball of string doubled my investment. The layered geometry of a tightly wound ball was wondrous to behold, whereas reeled-in string was nothing more than a lump on a cardboard core. The seasoned kite-flyer tied two and even three 250-foot balls together to get the kite to a respectable altitude.

The duration of the breeze could make or break a launch. In the absence of a good gust, I'd have to run with the kite, paying out string as I went. String burns on my fingers added pain to the pleasure of watching the kite gain altitude. Often, the launch would have to be scrubbed in order to add or subtract from the tail (torn handkerchief strips knotted together), or make some other critical adjustment. A roll of scotch tape in my pocket was handy for tissue paper tears (this was before the days of near-indestructible plastic or fabric kites in their myriad configurations). Those few kids who still fly kites today have a lot more leeway to perform feats like dueling and aerobatics. My overweening mission was simply to get—and keep—the kite up in the sky.

But sooner or later, all my paper flyers were goners. Flying a kite out as far as I did, I couldn't reel it in fast enough when peril was imminent. The string would get snagged or the wind would die. The string would break, a knot would untie, boredom would set in. Many a kite of mine wound up in arboreal clutches or hanging from a utility line. I also wrecked them in assorted blunt traumas. The flapping sound of a tail gone loco, the cruciform Icarus in uncontrollable spirals, the brittle *whump!*—and one more flight terminated with extreme prejudice.

In middle school, I sewed a windsock for a science project, but my interest was short-lived. Flying balsa planes and gliders consumed me for a while, until I came to the reluctant conclusion that the boy-hours spent building them didn't justify their often instantaneous demise. By way of compensation, my attention turned to model sailboats. In eighth-grade shop class, I made a racing sloop, hollowed out from a block of laminated pine, much in the manner of an authentic Chesapeake Bay log canoe. Mr. Carpenter, the eponymous shop teacher, had a boat I could copy. It sat atop a cabinet in his office (the same cabinet, where, in a matchbox, he kept the dried tip of his thumb as an object lesson to warn against carelessness with the table saw).

A boy—in those days, girls took Home Ec.—must have made the model sailboat a generation earlier and left it there. Single-masted and sawdust-becalmed, it was over two feet long, with a yellowing mainsail and jib, movable rudder, lead-weighted keel, and hand-filed brass fittings. It bespoke an era when school-kids worked more patiently and caused fewer disturbances. Mr. Carpenter seemed pleased that I wanted to undertake such a difficult project, but he warned me not to be in a rush about it. I had no easy time with the block of wood that was to become the hull. With a drawknife, I hacked away at its rectangularity until, after many shop periods and caliper measurings, I shaped the two longitudinal halves more or less symmetrically.

Then came the hard part: hollowing out the hull with a hammer and chisel. Since this was to be a functioning model, I needed to remove as much of the interior wood as possible, but one slip of the chisel, and I'd ruin the whole project. When the sharp steel tip got to within half an inch of the hull contour, I stopped chiseling, although Mr. Carpenter exhorted me to take off yet more wood. Instead, I began fashioning the deck from a thin sheet of poplar, and when I was done, I quickly glued and nailed it over the insufficiently hollow hull, thus forever hiding my pusillanimity. Mast, boom, and gunwale trim entailed hours of delicate carving; more than once, the sticks snapped in the vise and I had to start over. To outdo the old sailboat above the cabinet, I added a bowsprit and darkened the deck with mahogany stain. Lastly, I painted the hull with a high-gloss enamel, white above the waterline, red below. Though less perfect-looking than its inspiritor, my boat represented the pinnacle of my achievement in shop. In the remaining weeks of class, I hammered out a run-of-the-mill copper ashtray.

At home I sewed a set of sails from a defunct pillowcase and tied rigging lines with packing thread, and then I took my completed creation to the municipal duck pond. *Hillside*, as the boat was named (after my school), proved to be reasonably seaworthy despite its thick hull. A course could be set with the rudder, and the boat would sail straight. I'd run to the opposite bank to turn it around and, with a gentle shove, inaugurate yet another crossing. Yet by the time I was in tenth grade, *Hillside* stayed high and dry in its keel stand in the corner of my room. I had set a course to break free of anything that smacked of childhood. Simulacra of boats, airplanes, rockets, cars, and trains no longer appealed to me. Girls and reality were my pressing preoccupations.

Real sailing, for one, was on my agenda. Later in high school and through college, I had occasion to do a fair amount of it on freshwater lakes. One friend's family owned an old plywood Snipe, and on this I learned the basic skills. Its leaky cockpit required constant bailing, but the sailboat was so forgivingly solid that even when it was accidentally rammed into the dock, no noticeable damage occurred. In college, I sailed one-design-class Interclubs, which were lightweight fiberglass, round-bottomed, and tippy. Many carefree afternoons were spent on a glacial lake outside of Boston, where, under scudding cotton tufts, my sailing pals and I raced, played chicken, did mock battle, and pushed the envelope (and the regs) every way we could until John, the boathouse keeper, blew his air-horn fifteen minutes before sunset. This hands-on, seat-of-the-pants boatsmanship led me, many years later, to the sport of canoe-sailing.

But before that, a long period ensued in which my interaction with the wind was quite clearly in the doldrums. After college, I enlisted in the Navy, got married, moved to another city, pursued an art career, moved out to the country, and began raising a family. My father-in-law, a retired dentist, had a sailboat that I occasionally set foot on as a reluctant, nay, impressed crew member. Sailing with him was among the most unpleasant experiences I'd ever known; he was getting back at the world, I suppose, for years and years of cavity-filling.

By and by, I ceased actively thinking about sailing. At one point, I even considered putting *Hillside* in a rummage sale. But having rediscovered the old boat in the bottom of a box—its keel stand gone, its sails in tatters—my young son and daughter pleaded with me to fix it up and sail it for them. Thus encouraged, I sewed new sails, set the mast, and re-strung the rigging, and a restored *Hillside* voyaged across farm ponds to the delight of another generation. But the venerable model proved less watertight than it used to be; one gusty day it capsized and started to sink, in the middle of a pond, and, to my kids' amusement, I had to wade in, fully clothed, to the rescue. I couldn't allow an antique of my own creation to disappear so ignominiously. That was *Hillside*'s last voyage. Today, the old sloop sits in a replica keel stand on an end table in the living room, its patina of dust well earned.

Somewhere along the time-line of my second marriage, I acquired an old aluminum canoe, a Grumman seventeen-footer. Much as I enjoyed paddling it, I chose it because it could be converted to sail, that is, it came factory-equipped with mounting flanges for a mast and leeboards. In the late 1940s and through the 1950s, when canoe-sailing was in its heyday, the Metal Boat Company, a division of Grumman Aircraft Engineering Corporation, sold sailing kits consisting of a stubby lateen-rigged mast, a pair of retractable outrider stabilizers (leeboards), and a bolt-on sternpost and rudder. The sail was controlled with a simple sheet, the rudder with a rope-and-pulley system. The sport was considered an inexpensive and highly portable (atop a car) alternative to trailer sailboating. Summer camps offered it; freshwater recreation-seekers took it up in force (a fad that preceded the sit-down sailboard, a.k.a. the Sailfish and Sunfish).

But canoe-sailing had fallen into obscurity by the time I became interested in it. Conversion kits hadn't been manufactured in decades; in fact, Grumman *Aerospace* Corp. had stopped making canoes (though they still produced military aircraft). I searched intensively for an original Grumman sail kit—one to buy, one to copy, or parts thereof—and came up emptyhanded. Tens of thousands of the kits must have been sold, yet not a single one, it seemed, remained in existence. Fruitlessly, I canvased canoeists born long after canoe-sailing had been in vogue, who smiled at me indulgently: canoe-sailing was a cool idea, they all agreed, but they'd never heard of it (this was shortly before the advent of the World Wide Web).

One summer vacation, after I'd grown weary of paddling and was considering trading the canoe for something with a small outboard motor, I got a lucky break. On an inlet near Wilmington, North Carolina, I actually saw a person sailing a canoe. I couldn't believe my eyes; the way the craft glided along in the breeze utterly captivated me. In a series of private-property-invading trials and errors, I discovered the canoe, fully rigged, lying on its side on a dock. I returned with pencil, notebook, and tape measure, and, like an industrial spy, stole the proportions of that sailing kit right from under its owner's nose. I drew diagrams of everything, scribbling copious addenda, for I was convinced that I might never find another specimen.

That evening, flush with excitement, I also got the bright idea to check through the extensive collection of books on boating at the Wilmington Public Library. I was lucky there, too, finding a number of prints and illustrations, including an old Grumman publicity photo of a canoe regatta at a girl's camp, where every sail had a large cursive G at its apex and every girl—two to a canoe—was wearing a prim button-up sunsuit. I even found a book with an entire chapter devoted to canoe-sailing as practiced by nineteenth-century trappers on the northern lakes. Finally, I was in possession of actual information; the only thing left was to make my own sailing rig from scratch.

Having access to a local scrap yard full of odd piles of aluminum pipe and plate, I scrounged material for mast, mast brace, sail booms, leeboard brackets, sternpost, rudder mount, and various connectors and clamps. A machinist friend of mine, working from my drawings and measurements, created the requisite hardware. Meanwhile, I went to a lumberyard and picked out a mahogany plank, which I would saw and shape into leeboards and rudder. Before leaving Wilmington, I had gone to a marine supply store for braided line, sheaves, cleats, eyelets, and assorted stainless steel and nylon fasteners. From the Yellow Pages came the address of a sailmaker, from whom I ordered a custom sail. As it turned out, the sailmaker was a former canoe-sailing buff, so he gave me good advice about sail area (I had planned on too much) and control surface (too little this time).

The canoe sat on sawhorses in a barn while I completed its conversion. Mast brace, leeboard thwart, and rudder post were bolted on. The mast was stepped, leeboards and rudder polyurethaned, then mounted. A pair of rubber stretch cables kept each leeboard positioned downward (yet moveable when it hit something). Another rubber cable tensioned the steering lines extending from the rudder yoke. When the sail—the project's costliest component—arrived in the mail, I fastened it to the upper and lower booms with nylon wire ties, threaded its sheet through the sheaves, then pulled down triumphantly on its uphaul. The almost equilateral lateen rig shone like a movie screen above the complexities of aluminum and mahogany and rubber. I stood back and admired my handiwork. Limp and untested in the barn, it beckoned me toward the breezes of the local reservoir.

I was pleased to find that it sailed quite nicely. I had my share of capsizing, though; this was no foolproof sailcraft. A hard swing of the boom could send it heeling to the gunwale if the sheet—and the helmsman's posterior—wasn't adjusted quickly enough. When the canoe swamped, it tended to go all the way over, without a chance of being righted. I always wore a life vest and had a change of dry clothing on shore, toward which I would have to swim, pushing the upside-down craft ahead of me until I reached the shallows where I could stand up and manhandle it properly. The colder the water, the harder this was to accomplish—after one tipover, I'd usually have to call it a day. But my proficiency grew to the point where I could avoid all this, even in strong breezes. I learned how to sail with élan and stay dry. For several years, I kept up with the sport, however infrequently, although cartopping the canoe always meant a hassle, especially when I did it single-handedly.

Months go by, and the canoe rests upturned by the fishing deck, its wind-catching and water-guiding apparatus lashed above the thwarts. Since moving here, K and I have contented ourselves with watching other people's sailboats, those indolent descendants of the bygone fleets that practiced the disciplines of harvesting, commerce, and war. There was a time when harnessing the wind afloat meant the life or death of entire societies, and the political strength of nations. Nowadays, almost all such harnessing, when it occurs on the bay, is weekend play. Occasionally, I spot a restored old-timer with its canvas spread, and a lump comes to my throat. Common nostalgia, like the common cold, can't be avoided; it's amazing to think that only a few decades separate us from the way things used to be. The bugeyes, oyster skipjacks, and log canoes are living museums now. The closest we can come to them, experience-wise, is to go out on the water in our own little hybrid, whose maiden voyage on the Chesapeake is long overdue.

The perfect Saturday morning in midsummer arrives—the tide's high, the breeze is just right. Gingerly, my wife and I drag the canoe over the rip-rap down to the water—minimizing those aluminous scratchings that whitewater canoeists refer to as "Grumman Grip"—and tow it leftward through thigh-deep surf to the beach where I can rig it. So much time has passed, I've half-forgotten the procedure. I should have written it down; nobody in the whole world knew it except me. K offers encouragement as I slowly figure out what goes where. In our bathing suits, swim shoes, life vests, and chin-strapped sunhats, we must cut adventuresome, if peculiar, figures. She gets into the canoe and I push it out to where the leeboards only intermittently bang against the bottom. Clumsily, I ease myself aboard, shipping no small amount of water. Then we raise the sail.

The first thing that distinguishes this sailing episode from all previous ones is the bay's tumult. From the bluff, the water looked placid, but here, at flotation level a hundred yards offshore where crab pots are strewn to a depth of perhaps ten feet, we're in a moderate swell, a boat-rocker that in itself is a force to be reckoned with. As the breeze pushes us outward, K and I are somewhat apprehensive until we realize that we're not sliding under the waves each time the bow dips. Up we come, again and again. Exuberance sets in, once we get used to it.

However deftly I handle rudder-line and sheet, every successive wave nudges the rudder of its own accord. With a full lateen and the steadiest of winds, we roll and toss. Reservoir sailing, for all its unpredictability, was puddle-smooth compared to this. Our slender craft no longer conveys that flying feeling, but wallows, albeit lightly and directionally, through the chop. Speed can be gauged only relative to the crab pot buoys; more than once we brush up against one, though I'm trying like the devil to steer in between.

A waterman's workboat advances toward our lee, its helmsman seemingly oblivious to our Sybaritic meandering. It's just an ordinary white workboat, the kind so frequently seen from the bluff that I don't bother to scrutinize it through binoculars anymore. Here in the watery milieu, it appears larger than life, with stained freeboard and sputtering engine and blue exhaust. Crab pots are stacked on the roof, giving it a top-heavy look despite its wide beam. We wave, and one of the coveralled watermen raises his hand marginally. Okay, so we're a pain in the neck, but aren't we entitled to use these waters, too?

Two other workboats are approaching. Perhaps we had better get out of their space, let them earn their living in peace. A jibe gradually conveys us beyond the styrofoam buoy field into deeper water. We look back to the house, which appears diminutive and mostly concealed behind verdure. A mile or so in either direction are a pair of World War II–era observation towers, spread-legged wooden structures once painted white, now decaying platforms for an automated beacon of some sort. The coastline distends before us—to the left, the bluff tapering beyond our northward neighbors' place, and to the right, the bayfront residences of Tolchester above a patchwork of timber bulkheading or rip-rap or nothing at all.

The wind has picked up a bit, and now the question is: should we try to sail across the channel? We debate the safety of setting a course for buoy #31 on the far side, tacking around it and working our way back. Although no shipping traffic is in sight, pleasure boats are streaming past, one after another. In this breeze, we could cut across in ten minutes. We're both aware of the risk, but we're pretty pumped up—we've come this far, we might as well go a little farther (my original plan to sail clear over to Pooles Island is, as I see now, way too ambitious).

As we venture into the deep-draft realm, a substantial trough further tosses us. A two-foot chop is all well and good for a boat with more than six inches of freeboard, but for us, the sawn-in-half milk jug bailer is getting a workout. I'm having to allow a little less heel on the reaches, even though K is a fearless first mate and a ready shifter of ballast. We're making progress, exhilaratingly so, but it is a long ten minutes as the parade of watercraft crosses or passes us. A spinnaker-powered cruiser overtakes us, looking stable as an aircraft carrier, its crew members waving their palms lèse-majesté-style. Yeah, we're tiny compared with you, but we're doing fine, we wave back. Several powerboats zoom up from the north and south, and pass, full tilt, too close for comfort, causing me to change course to deal with their wakes. Thanks a lot, assholes! More bailing.

Maybe the channel crossing wasn't such a good idea after all, but it's too late to turn back. We are nearly at the buoy, which towers over our sea-level perspective, its green paint streaked with white. A pair of resident cormorants departs as we sail to within fifty feet. Tacking around it, I'm giddy with adventure and tell K, "One day we'll own a real sailboat, sail all the way to Baltimore, all the way to the mouth of the bay, Bermuda even, and this outing will seem like child's play."

Ever the supportive and practical mate, she smiles enthusiastically, then suggests that for the moment we concentrate on making it back to the beach.

Re-entering the danger zone, we keep close tabs on the pleasure boats coming our way. Two offshore racing-type powerboats give us wide berth, shooting rooster tails. The wind angle is forcing us to cross the channel obliquely; it'll take more time to get home. One motor cruiser, a hefty one, seems to be heading straight for us. Surely the guy's gonna veer away any second—he has to—but the big vee-plashing prow keeps bearing down. I try holding a sharper angle to the wind, but we're sitting ducks. Bigger, louder—C'mon, dude, can't you see us? The menace blots out the pretty panorama. Now panicky, we wave our arms and yell like crazy. *Hey, look in front of you! Hey, we're right here!* Just as our lives are about to parade before our eyes, the danger swerves, digging a mountainous wake that almost swamps us.

K and I get a good glimpse of the man at the helm, a heavyset sixtyish fellow with a loud shirt and a drink in hand. And he is waving down at us, smiling!

Still gasping for breath, we are less than amused. He probably hasn't meant us any harm; he's merely slipping along in a happy groove, appreciating the horsepower at his fingertips and apparently not paying too much attention to where he's going. Maybe he expected us to tack, though given the disparity in speeds, it wouldn't have done much good. Maybe he saw us all along and wanted a closer look. Maybe he's just a lousy driver. Whatever, he gives us a serious scare—and food for thought.

K and I sail the remainder of the channel without further incident, but we are spooked by—and wiser for—our near miss. In retrospect, I see that we've been extremely fortunate. We had no contingency plan for a capsize, no chance of righting our canoe, little chance of swimming home with it, no hand-held VHF, nothing to make us brighter or easier to spot from the bridge of another faster vessel. There hasn't been time to go out in the canoe again, but when we do, we plan to remedy these deficiencies. And I think it's safe to say that we'll stick with the wind closer to shore.

chapter

6

In 1926, a Wilmington businessman named John M. Mendinhall acquired inside information that a bridge across Chesapeake Bay was under consideration, with its eastern terminus adjacent to the popular Tolchester Beach and Amusement Park. Plans for the bridge, the longest of its kind anywhere in the world, had not yet been made public but were due to be unveiled shortly. In addition to being a bank president, gentleman farmer, and former Lieutenant-Governor of Delaware, Mendinhall was also a yachtsman with an intimate knowledge of the upper bay, and particularly its eastern shore.

Quickly and without fanfare, Mendinhall, together with a business associate named Harry M. Pierce (a chief engineer at Du Pont), arranged to purchase four farms surrounding the Tolchester park, totaling in excess of a thousand acres, with over two miles of waterfront. The bridge terminus would fall squarely on this property. Mendinhall's plan was to subdivide the area nearest the park into hundreds of residential lots, leaving a wide thoroughfare that fanned out for toll booths, and, if all went well, to continue to carve up the whole tract as the bridge's transference of wealth and industry from the western shore dictated.

Tolchester Estates, Inc., Mendinhall and Pierce's development corporation, operated through established realty agencies in Wilmington and Baltimore but did the majority of its business from a sales office right at the edge of the amusement park. By steamer alone, some ten to fifteen thousand people arrived daily during the summer season. Add to this figure the hordes of visitors who would cross via the bridge, and it becomes clear why

Mendinhall and Pierce believed themselves to be on the verge of a bonanza.

A brochure was distributed, the cover of which depicted an artist's rendition of the eight-mile span with a bay steamer passing underneath a raised drawbridge section. *"The Signatures of Pres.* Coolidge and Governor Ritchie *made* This Bridge Possible!" crows the future-as-fait-accompli caption. In the foreground, happy bathers and boaters, primitively out of scale, loll beside the steamboat pier. Perpendicular to the beach are two mammoth waterslides dumping thrill seekers right into the surf. The pier leads to an esplanade that features a twin-towered pavilion, and behind it, on the bluff, a verandah-skirted hotel. At the edge of the illustration is the park's renowned roller coaster, Whirl-Pool Dips, with its many flags gaily fluttering. The illustration both simplifies and heightens reality: from an engineering viewpoint the bridge looks improbable, while the water, minimally limned, appears smooth as glass.

The brochure's center spread is an airbrushed aerial photograph of the newly purchased four-farm tract. In it, the bridge is not pictured per se; instead, a large white arrow ("Eastern Shore terminus of the new Chesapeake Bay Bridge as published") points to a section of beach several hundred yards north of the pier. What is pictured, however, is a grid of streets depicting the development-to-be along the bluff. At the page margin, the copy is in keeping with the speculative optimism of the roaring twenties:

> As for the owners and developers of Tolchester Estates, your success will be their success in that part of Tolchester Estates which is now being sold to you in building lots, while but a small portion of their entire land holdings at Tolchester, is at present the choicest and most valuable section, being that part which adjoins the Tolchester Park, the pier, the State Concrete Road, and right at the bridge terminus (as published) in the *Baltimore Sun* of July 31st, 1928; therefore, if the entire holdings of Tolchester Estates, Inc. are to be developed and sold,

your lots and all the lots now being sold at Tolchester Estates, must first advance and appreciate in value. In other words—Make you Money . . .

The usual business forecast is made in the light of the past. But the future of Tolchester Estates cannot be foretold on the basis of traditional signs—with the building of this great bridge (as proposed) that will transport hundreds of thousands speedily and cheaply to and from Tolchester, the conservative growth of the past will be overshadowed by the tremendous growth of the future.

Our advice to you, then, is investigate, buy and wait—for the secret of a million fortunes is, invest a few hundred dollars in land at the right time at the right place.

Cut Out This Coupon—and Mail it Today . . .

According to the brochure, lots were to be sold in increments of 20 × 100 feet, with "10-foot sidewalk free," and title guaranteed. Lot prices were $79.50, $159.00, and $250.00, depending on proximity to the water and the park. "Small down payment, easy terms" were promised. In the bullish market, this was perfectly pitched pay-as-you-go aimed at the wage-earning masses, a chance for upward mobility by way of a toehold in the shadow of an established resort. Additionally, there were advertised "a limited number of business locations on the concrete highway."[1]

Mendinhall and Pierce wasted no time moving six pre-existing summer cottages inland from various points along the bluff and re-siting them on staked-out streets to give the illusion of a development already in place. In one of these cottages lived the resident engineer and his family; his job was the mowing of the former farm fields and the spreading of street gravel dredged from the shallows of the beach. An article in the *Kent News* on August 21, 1926, heralded the grand opening:

At Tolchester, Chesapeake Bay, Kent County, Maryland, within a comparatively short time, will be reared one of the biggest pleasure resorts and summer residential sections in the

history of Delmarva Penninsula, if plans of the Tolchester
Estates, Inc., materialize.

Announcement was made by interests of the Tolchester
Estates of the acquiring of a vast area of farm land comprising
about 1,200 acres, in which is embraced 16 acres of lake water,
to be developed under present plans, into a yachting harbor. It
is proposed to transform the entire plot into a beautiful playground, with residential sections of 3,000 homes, golf course,
club house, parks, board walk and pavilions. . . .

That the climate and water at Tolchester are healthful is
contained in a report following a careful survey of the vast tract.

A Topographical Study has also been made, which reveals
the midland drainage to be of the best, thus providing only
nourishing soil for shrubbery, trees, growing vines, and other
foliage.

It was further stressed that it is the purpose of the Tolchester Estates, Inc., to sell the home sites only to reputable
people, with restrictions to a certain class of improvements. It
is planned to dedicate certain parks in honor of the residents.
Trees will be planted along the streets and every modern improvement made.

The Tolchester Estates are 65 miles South of Wilmington,
21 miles from Baltimore. Good roads and transportation facilities add to the importance of the place. . . .

The new harbor development will provide every facility for
yacht clubs, boat houses and suitable cottages.

For several years, the sales office at the edge of the park did a
brisk business. Revelers—accompanied, likely as not, with someone they wanted to impress—came in straight from the Whirl-
Pool Dips or one of the other exciting ten-cent rides. Cash in the
pocket was painlessly exchanged for twenty feet of dreams,
twenty feet that yearned to be added to—doubled, if not trebled
or quadrupled—as more money was earned. Ostensibly, land
speculation on so modest a scale couldn't go wrong. For the creation of a "million fortunes," this was indeed the right place and
the right time.

But the bridge was never built. Instead, economically speak-

ing, one shoe dropped—the Crash of 1929—and then the other—
the ensuing Great Depression. In 1931, in the Maryland House of
Delegates, the bridge proposal lost by one vote.[2] When it became
clear that the idea would never be revived, lot sales all but came
to a halt, only to resume in 1939, after John M. Mendinhall had
died and a disillusioned Harry M. Pierce had sold his interest.
Disposing of much of the farmland and dividing several large
parcels among family members, the Mendinhall heirs managed
to continue lot sales as the ravages of the Depression eased.
But the development would remain small, ancillary to the
amusement park, which in itself retained formidable drawing
power even though no golf course, boardwalk, or yacht basin had
appeared.

Not until 1952 was the initial span of the present William
Preston Lane, Jr., Memorial Bridge completed, the extension, to
the south, of Routes 50 and 301 across the bay between Annapolis and Kent Island. This was the bridge that, ironically, sounded
the death knell for Tolchester Park, in that it helped to convey
vacationers straight to the Atlantic beaches. On a further ironic
note, Kent Island has suffered the very overdevelopment that
Mendinhall and Pierce had unwittingly projected for Tolchester
in their quest for a windfall.

A surveyor's map dated April 1927 shows the initial version of
Tolchester Estates, with space for the bridge toll plaza along the
northern extremity of the amusement park, and a narrow band
of vacant land, extending for eleven blocks, designated for the
boardwalk at bluff's edge. East of the park, running toward
and parallel to its border, the proposed streets are named for
trees: Cedar, Willow, Maple, Poplar, Linden, Oak, and Elm—all
of which terminate at Montgomery Avenue, the grand gateway
that was to lead away from the bridge. On the far side of Montgomery, at an angle, are other avenues named after counties:
Harford, Baltimore, Cumberland, and Queen Anne (the exception is Bayview, closest to the water); perpendicular to these,
south to north, are streets named for states: Montana, Wyoming,
Iowa, and so on. Trees, counties, states—all very complementary

and middlebrow, as if the methodology of a Calvin Coolidge had set them there.

By the late 1960s, several generations of buyers and inheritors, reacting to the exigencies of the Depression, World War II, and the demise of the amusement park, had consolidated many of the original twenty-, forty-, and eighty-foot lots into a hodgepodge of slightly larger ones. The cottages and bungalows that did get built were universally modest. A small fire station was erected. While the subdivision's name, Tolchester Estates, remained, the development corporation was all but defunct, although it wouldn't be formally dissolved until 1983. Meanwhile, the Mendinhall heirs conveyed all public rights-of-way to the fledgling Tolchester Community Association, which in turn deeded the main routes to Kent County for purposes of upkeep. Streets on which no houses had been built reverted to nature. A proposed landing strip for private planes was voted down. By the early 1970s, after the remains of the amusement park had been sold to a marina developer and subsequently removed, the community association rehabbed its old fire station as a meeting hall.

Today, the community association struggles to justify its existence, convening every other month or so in its cinderblock headquarters. The annual door-to-door membership drive (yearly dues: $25.00) is suppported by fewer than half of the residents. In addition to holding sparsely attended meetings, the association also maintains a beach and boat ramp at the end of Ohio, as well as an entrance sign flanked by ornamental grasses at the corner of Elm and State Route 21. Bingo, dances, rummage sales, potlucks, and Tai Chi are still held in the old hall, but the building was recently burglarized and the money box stolen, so bingo is on hold for the time being.

The present community, with a summer population of around five hundred, and a winter population of less than half that number, is a commerce-free, unincorporated sodality of mostly unpaved streets and street-ends. No sidewalks—ten feet wide, imagine!—were ever built, although there are plenty of drainage ditches. A number of the less-traveled rights-of-way, the ones that haven't gone back to briar and brush, are informally claimed, via the riding mower, as extensions of back yards.

In my possession, courtesy of a neighbor who is a direct descendant of John M. Mendinhall, are two original Tolchester Estates sales contracts, dating from the 1940s, for the three lots comprising the seven-tenths of an acre on which our house and outbuildings are situated.

The more I study the documents—each is printed on a single sheet, front and back—the more I glimpse a past that has vanished utterly, like the park and the proposed bridge. In Old English typeface, "Tolchester Estates, Inc., Grantor," sets as somber a tone as a last will and testament. Lots 2, 3, and 4, of block 1-A in Plat #3 are hereby solemnly sold. In the 1927 survey map, these oversize lots—each 100 feet at the street and extending more than 200 feet to the water's edge[3]—are located at the extreme northern tip of the development, with equally large parcels to either side, but none behind.

The three lots have been purchased on a time payment plan tailored to the war years. The earliest of the two sales contracts, dated June 14, 1941, stipulates that the $900 price for lot 2 be met in the following manner: "$90 deposited herewith, and the balance of $810 as follows: $15 on the 3rd of each and every month until the full amount of $900 is paid, with 5% interest per annum added on all delinquent monthly payments, and on all payments after June 14th, 1943." In a nutshell, this is a four-and-a-half year loan with the first two years interest-free. The second contract, dated December 9, 1944, combines lots 3 and 4 at a discounted price of $1600, with proportionally identical terms.

The buyer in the first contract is one James Thomas Blackiston, possessor of a signature, in black ink, worthy of inscription alongside that of John Hancock. Its flourish bespeaks a young man who is sure of himself, fluidly so. At the lower left front page, along the dotted line for Witness, is the signature of one Nanette L. Roche. Hers is up-and-down orotund, also in black, with a deliberate enlargement that indicates Virgoan carefulness and perhaps also punctuality. Two-and-a-half years later, on the second contract, the buyers are listed as James Thomas Blackiston and Nanette Roche Blackiston. A newlyweds' sanguinity suffuses both signatures—his in purple ink, hers in blue-black with the fountain pen pressed more firmly than before and the E at the end of Roche cut short so that her new last name gets on the line. Under "Buyers' Address," she lists a different one in Baltimore from the one he had registered in 1941. Yes, they've married, moved, bought a triple bayfront parcel, a nice big one, right outside the hurly-burly amusement park, and the war is winding down. In all likelihood, the young couple has been crossing the bay between Baltimore and Tolchester for years. On one such steamer excursion, they may have fallen in love. He's been in uniform—a junior officer in the Navy—and she's been on the homefront; together, they've committed themselves to building a waterfront retreat. If this isn't a personification of the American Dream, I don't know what is.

But turn over an original Tolchester Estates sales contract, and a darker story emerges. The back page is headed **RESTRICTIONS**, in boldface caps that give due warning of the fine print that follows. There are eight enumerated paragraphs, and they start out innocuously enough.

Paragraphs #1 and #2 state that all dwellings must be set back from the road at least ten feet; all garages set back not less than seventy feet; all business buildings need prior approval from the Grantor. The house setback is consistent with chock-a-block residential density of the time—a cross-bay ripple, perhaps, of the row houses Baltimore is famous for. The garage setback is a carryover from earlier days when stables and carriage barns were positioned far to the rear of residences. In the 1940s, rural Kent County still has no building codes, so these arbitrary standards are legally binding. The development corporation's demand for approval of business structures no doubt refers to the double and quadruple lots on the perimeter of the amusement park and along the boardwalk, the idea being to eliminate commercial unsightliness.

Paragraph #3 stipulates that no privy can be built except with written permission from the Grantor, nor can swine be kept on the premises. Since this is an up-to-date community, the installation of indoor plumbing is recommended, although Tolchester Estates, Inc., makes no provisions for a central sewer or water hookup (what will evolve over the years is a glut of wells and septic tanks—a befouling, bay-fouling overload that won't be remedied until the mid-1990s). As for pigs, besides smelling bad, they have a tendency to wander onto streets and wallow in ditches. The Grantor emphatically won't countenance that. Also, the paragraph states that no "nuisance of any kind shall be maintained or allowed thereon, nor any use thereof made nor permitted which shall be noxious or dangerous to health." A blanket clause, to be sure, but one that seems vague enough to permit leeway in its interpretation. After all, one person's nuisance may be another's pride and joy.

Paragraph #4 takes a swerve into the realm of the despotic. It states, in paraphrase, that all covenants and agreements shall remain in force and are binding any time the lot is conveyed, which is pretty much boilerplate for saying that Tolchester Estates, Inc., intends to keep things as they are in perpetuity—a sentiment more appropriate for a cemetery than a housing development. The growing pains and unforeseen difficulties attending such an unplanned community—starting from scratch, no less—seem not to be taken into consideration. Likewise, adjustment of the community's charter and character may be nigh impossible. Yet the fine print says it plainly: change, if it comes at all, is to be allowed only with the "mutual consent of the said Grantor or its succcessor and the owner or owners." In other words, Tolchester Estates, Inc., retains full veto power over the future.

Paragraph #5 gets down to specifics again: "No trees, hedge, shrubbery or blind of any kind will be permitted that will in any way obstruct the view of the bay from any lot-owner." A regulation like this can only be interpreted as anti-privacy, not to mention anti-vegetation, considering the flat topography behind the bluff and the plethora of inland-running streets. This probably explains why many of the older trees in the contemporary community have a stunted, sawed-off appearance, and why there are few mature hedges. Big Brother—for surely this restriction signifies a coercive mindset—reserves the right to sit in his touring phaeton all the way over on Cedar Street and cop a view of the water (and while he's at it, keep tabs on neighborhood mores). Big Brother continues: "the Tolchester Estates [can] order the said obstructions to be trimmed or removed or enter premises to do so, for the general welfare of the community." Thus concludes the paragraph, with no mention of owners' appeals, beautification committees, or public hearings. If Tolchester Estates, Inc., deems a tree should be removed, down it goes. Property thus controlled is not exactly private. "General welfare" administered by those with absolute legal power is similarly dispensed by jackbooted thugs across the ocean, against whom freedom-loving Americans are currently struggling. The goals of the nation at war appear in stark contrast to this liberty-depriving clause that seeks to render a man's castle not only transparent, but trespassable as well.

Paragraph #6 further details the erosion of property owners' rights. "The Tolchester Estates, Inc., reserve [sic] the right to enter upon the premises, herein mentioned, at any time prior to the erection of a dwelling thereon, and grade the same, placing soil thereon or removing soil therefrom, and to cut grass, remove weeds and plant and cultivate flowers, shrubs and trees thereon, and at any time to enter along the back line thereof to install and maintain or license others to install and maintain thereon wires and apparatus above and below the ground for electric light or telephone, or both for general use."

Hasn't the inventive legal mind that drew up this convoluted proscription ever heard of easements? In most instances, utilities make separate contracts with property owners: service in exchange for permission to run lines. Not so in Tolchester Estates. As for free landscaping, that sounds like a major plus, but it's not spelled out specifically. It could mean, "we're dumping this pile of dirt in your yard for reasons that are none of your business," or "we're removing your topsoil, and you'll have to buy it back from us." Overall, the message seems to be, "If you don't keep your lot the way we like it, we'll come in and correct it to our specifications, *but even if you do everything right, we're still going to come in and mess around, just to show you who's boss!*"

But paragraph #7 is the kicker. "At no time shall the above described lot, or any part thereof, or any building thereon erected be sold, leased or transferred to, or occupied by any one who is not of the White race, nor [sic] of a Gentile faith. This provision, however, not to include occupancy by servants, or any employee of owner or occupant of said lot."

In addition to being told all the things a Tolchesterite can't do, here's a dictum spelling out what a Tolchesterite can't be! Such restrictions were not unusual in real estate contracts of the era—they continued right up until after the Fair Housing Act of 1968 and subsequent laws were put in force—but in a decidedly modest community composed of mainly twenty-foot lots, this is Jim Crow and anti-Semitism at its most virulent. The high-handed exception for servants can only be interpreted as a conceit of upper-crust Wilmington, for few, if any, Tolchesterites would have the means to employ such persons. From a contemporary viewpoint, the whole premise is difficult to understand. What about all those automobiles coming over the proposed bridge? Non-whites and non-Gentiles drove cars, didn't they? Yet this stricture fitted perfectly with the admissions policy at Tolchester Park, where African Americans were denied entrance except for *one day a year*, following Labor Day, when the park was on the verge of closing for the season. (Jews enjoyed their uncontested mufti as white citizens.)

Paragraph #8 sneaks in one final abrogation of individual rights, more turgidly—and thus harder to decipher—than the others. "It is further agreed that the said grantee shall not assign the within contract without the consent of the Grantor in writing, and that no sign or any description shall be placed on the premises for a period of five years without permission in writing from the Grantor."

This is a truly scary prospect. Lots can't be re-sold to just any-one. If you, as lot owner, want to—or need to—bow out of the Tolchester scene, you may be in for trouble. Big Brother has to approve of your buyer. What's more, for five years, you can't put up a For Sale sign without Big Brother's permission. You can't put up any sign at all, not even a five-cents-a-glass lemonade sign. And why shouldn't there be signs? Is there concern for awkward lettering, misspelled words? Are tag sales forbidden? Is there fear of unbridled cottage industry—bird houses, wishing wells, crocheted items? This stifling of free expression can have only one impetus: realty paranoia.

Tolchester Estates, Inc., didn't want purchasers to turn around and become sellers, not while the marketing push was on. Given the Depression years and, later, the War, with housing starts slow, this was the best way to suppress new lot-owners' cold feet. After owning a lot for five years—and most likely adding to it—buyers would be more inclined to erect some kind of struc-ture, however humble, than to sell. Meanwhile, the developers wanted nothing to distract the eye, or instill doubt in the heart, of a potential customer. This concluding paragraph is just one more attempt by the Grantor to consolidate absolute control.

John M. Mendinhall's and Harry M. Pierce's disappointment over the voted-down bridge must have been enormous. Monitor-ing the Depression as it worsened, they must have understood that profits would be severely curtailed. As the lean years rolled by, what they probably desired most was to keep their shirts. Gradually, the fate of Tolchester Estates was loosed from its original bylaws as it evolved into an eclectic, if spotty, commu-nity of seasonal and year-round residences. I would suspect that few, if any, lot owners felt oppressed or stymied by the back page of the sales contract. If anything, the restrictions probably bol-stered buyer self-esteem. At any rate, by the time the Mendin-hall heirs pulled away from their role as overseers, most of the small print seems to have gone largely unheeded.

I have it on good authority that Nanette Roche Blackiston and her husband John enjoyed their three woodsy, bluff-edge lots overlooking the bay. In 1949, the couple built a small cinder-block summer house with a sleeping attic—the seminal section of the rambling dwelling K and I occupy today. After John died, Mrs. Blackiston married a man named Seitz, who added on to both sides of the house and did some major remodeling. Decades later, after his death, she continued to spend summers and temperate weekends here until she grew too old to take care of the place. On the verge of entering a nursing home, she sold it to the husband and wife from whom we bought it, who added more to the structure (again at both ends), winterized it, and lived here year-round for eleven years.

The extensive, orderly, working-class vacation utopia that was intended for Tolchester metamorphosed into something much smaller and looser than the 1927 survey map hinted at. A few elderly original owners are still around to tell the oral history of the old days, but most of the current residents give the impression of knowing nothing of the past that can't be gleaned from their satellite dishes. This middling generation coexists with detachments of bored, skateboarding teenagers. There are also babies and, of course, dogs. Cluttered front and back yards give testament to a wholly deregulated sense of community. Realtors' signs hang with impunity. Marina folk shuttle between their fiberglass boats and asbestos-sided ranchers. In the area where the amusement park used to be, a community of larger, boxier homes, known as Tolchester Heights, clusters along a horseshoe-shaped road that terminates in a cul-de-sac. Everybody's, like, making do and getting by; perpetuity has become passé.

When I decide to build a garage, it's long past the era of the seventy-foot setback, and it's a good thing, too, because our property lies within what is referred to as a "Critical Area." Defining it as "irreplaceable habitat . . . crucial to the protection of the Chesapeake Bay and its tributaries," the Kent County Planning Commission sets the rules now; any type of new construction has to have a minimum one-hundred-foot buffer from mean high tide. Subtracting one hundred feet from the already severely subtracted-from coast leaves us no place for the garage except in *front* of the house. This is fine with me—I see it as a belated thumbing-my-nose at the pernicious contractual proscriptions of yore.

I get involved in another kind of contract: a builder's contract, which, as it turns out, becomes a comedy of errors in many acts. The first error is that I decide to hire a pole-building firm to erect the garage instead of doing it myself. Pole construction, utilizing load-bearing, evenly spaced, pressure-treated wooden poles, eliminates the need for a masonry foundation. With four owner-built homes under my belt, I'm no greenhorn at this sort of thing, but I've grown chary of do-it-yourself construction projects when they fall under the purlieus of nit-picking local codes. Building inspectors can be the nemesis of free expression with a hammer and saw, and although it's been years, I still have nightmares about dealing with them.

My plan, therefore, is to contract out the whole kit-and-kaboodle. In magazine classifieds—here's my second error—I keep coming across pole-builders' advertisements that appeal to my ex-builder's sense of detachment. Why bust your butt constructing an outbuilding—a barn, a garage, a shed, a workshop, a stable—when one can be erected on site, with quality and savings guaranteed, if you call certain toll-free numbers? Why, indeed! Each number, when dialed, yields a female voice that takes your name, address, home phone, and the dimensions of the structure you have in mind. A week later, you receive a photo brochure of the most attractive utility buildings imaginable, plus a typed, unsigned sales contract. Two weeks after that, a follow-up phone call from a faraway salesman responds "No problem" to your every query. You're urged to return the signed contract with a down payment before the proverbial price increase goes into effect.

I call five such firms and collect as many ready-to-go contracts and disembodied sales pitches. Of these, I choose an Indiana firm, Polecat Structures, Inc., that promises to begin building the garage within six weeks—"eight weeks at the outside,

because orders are coming in faster than reproducing rabbits."
The hyperbolic salesman introduces himself as Rob and grows
schmoozier by the minute. According to Rob, Polecat has four
construction crews staying busy in nineteen states, each com-
pleting a structure in an average of three working days, dotting
the countryside with the company's award-winning product. In
his every utterance, he convinces me of Polecat's irreproachable
renown. We fax building plans back and forth until, sure of what
I'm getting, I forward a signed contract—plus a check for more
than fifteen hundred dollars. Then I sit back and wait for this
miraculous garage-by-fingertips to materialize well before cold
weather sets in.

As the weeks go by, I turn my attention to the preliminaries
on this end. The garage will fit tightly between an as-yet-unbuilt
walkway, a tangled row of trees, a storage shed, and the length of
a parked car from the road. I complete the pea-gravel-and-rail
walkway and trim back the overhanging branches. With a homemade transit, I check the site grade for levelness, spreading dirt
as necessary. I'm tempted to set up batter boards and string out
the 24' by 26' footprint myself—it would be half an afternoon's
work. I could also order poles from the local lumberyard and get
busy with a two-handled post-hole digger. Planting the poles by
myself wouldn't take long. But no, I've got other work to do. The
contract specifically states "***Building Cost Included***"—
this is what I'm shelling out all the money for. I'm only required
to provide "four (4) stakes marking the corners of the building . . .
in the exact location [I] wish the building to be built." Still, it's
frustrating to watch day after day of good weather slip by.

Eight weeks, ten weeks pass. Well schooled in builder's patience, I don't mind waiting a little longer. Rob said that Polecat's mid-Atlantic schedule might be backlogged; there's no
point in raising a stink yet. After another two weeks, though, I
venture a toll-free call. Autumn is waning and the days are getting chilly. In my experience, frozen ground is not conducive to
digging holes. Inquiring for Rob, I'm told he's temporarily inca-
pacitated. "He's had a heart attack, I think," says the indifferent

receptionist. My call is transferred to another salesman, Duane. During the time I'm on Hoosier-elevator-music hold, I feel the anger rising within. Suddenly, I don't care what their excuse is, a contract's a contract. I've handed over a hefty sum of money and been shown nothing in return. When Duane gets on the line, I let him have it full blast.

"Okay, Duane, ¿qué pasa? Polecat's had my paperwork and my deposit check for twelve weeks. Where's the damn garage?"

Duane professes to know nothing about my dealings with Rob, nor is he able to retrieve any pertinent information via computer other than a record of my check having been received. Offhandedly, Duane informs me that Rob has had a mental breakdown and is no longer with the company. "But the receptionist said . . ." Stress from overwork, apparently. He just got nuttier and nuttier, and eventually went off his rocker. Not to worry, though, Duane assures me, I'm not the only customer affected. Some of the scheduling may be out of kilter. It's disconcerting to hear him go on like this—as if he does it every day. But he promises to get my order straightened out; annoyingly, he insists on going back to square one, asking me once again to go over all the details.

More faxing, more firming up. I'm committed to an additional two hundred dollars for selecting green shingles, which aren't an option in the standard package. No problem, says Duane. Polecat handles special orders all the time. Duane spells out the contract terms with much more precision than Rob ever did. As each step is completed, I'm to write a check to cover that particular cost. What I have to wait for now—after receiving a copy of the scale-drawn plans and okaying them—are these three preliminaries: the delivery of the basic lumber materials, the arrival of the roof trusses, and a visit from the hole-driller. Shortly thereafter, the construction crew will show up. They'll need two days at most to frame, side, and roof a building of this size, he says, and as soon as their work is finished, the overhead door installer will come. "All in all, it won't take very long, trust me."

"What about the cold weather?" I ask.

Chuckling long distance, Duane informs me that Polecat

crews work straight through the winter. "Heck, they built a two-hundred-foot chicken house in a Minnesota blizzard last January."

So six more weeks go by, and not a single delivery. Winter begins moderately, with plenty of good days for working outdoors, each one tugging at the sleeve of my hammer arm. My every reflex strains to get started. Instead, I'm flexing my fingers, dialing Polecat's 800 number, demanding updates. But I'm no longer put through to Duane—he was merely a drummer-up of business, a honey-tongued front man. Instead, I'm connected to an assistant foreman in production, who congenially informs me that everything is proceeding on schedule. When the architectural drawings arrive in the mail, I check them over—they look fine—and express-mail them back, thinking it'll save time. More weeks go by. Then one subfreezing day at dusk, a flatbed tractor-trailer arrives with the lumber strapped in two large bundles which are lowered to the front yard by a radio-controlled crane. I'm so grateful to see tangible proof of Polecat's existence that I don't mind forking over the two thousand dollars-plus that the driver is authorized to collect.

In another couple of weeks, the trusses arrive hanging upside down upon a custom-made gooseneck trailer. Eager to do something, I help the driver unload them. On the trailer, too, is a Bobcat with a rotary auger to drill the post holes. An afternoon of full sun has momentarily thawed the ground, so with my assistance, the staking-out process goes quickly. As the twelve holes are consecutively spun out to four feet in depth, I'm whistling the ballad about the steam hammer versus John Henry. When the driver is loaded up and ready to leave, I write out another check, this one for slightly under one thousand dollars. From the configuration of holes and the tarpaulin-covered mound of lumber, I can almost will the garage into existence, its walls and gable ends and single sixteen-foot door that will open at the touch of a button, in place and painted and in use.

But for some reason, the construction crew is delayed (I wonder why I'm not surprised). I consult with the production foreman, who tells me that the crew has already been dispatched.

Once they finish a job in Ohio, they'll be on their way. They should arrive in Tolchester by the end of the week. They don't. The following week, I call the foreman again and get a similar answer. They'll be here toward the end of the week, or at the *very latest*, the first of the coming week. Five such weeks of unrequited anticipation go by. Finally, it dawns on me that I'm the recipient of a long-distance lie. The frustrating truth is that Polecat has no plans to send a construction crew to Maryland. For four thousand, five hundred dollars, I got a pile of lumber and twelve holes in the front yard.

K thinks I've been duped. Winter is almost over and there's snow on the ground. My builder's patience looks stupider by the minute. In the next series of phone calls to Polecat, I vent my spleen to the point where the foreman refuses to communicate with me anymore. I try to reach the company president, but he's never there. I've half a mind to drive to Indiana and personally straighten things out, preferably with an AK-47. K recommends the legal route instead; she urges me, for starters, to read the small print on the contract:

TIME FOR COMPLETION: The project shall be completed in a timely manner except that the Contractor shall not be responsible for delays due to acts of God, inclement weather, strikes, lockouts, material shortages, lack of availability of utility services, fire, storm, theft, vandalism or other causes beyond [the contractor's] control . . .

Although the Hoosier legalmeisters appear to have covered all contingencies, I won't give up. At my request, our lawyer drafts a demand letter to the company president, stating that if construction isn't started within fourteen days—the expiration date of the Kent County building permit—Polecat Structures, Inc., will be sued for breach of contract. There's nothing "timely" in stretching a six-week completion date to six months. Abandoning my telephone technique, I fire off a fax exhorting the president to avoid the upcoming legal brouhaha by sending in a crew right away. Like the lawyer, I receive no reply, but late in the afternoon on the day before the permit is to expire and the wheels of justice are poised to turn, a battered, salt-besmirched van with Indiana plates and a ladder tied to its roof drives up with two scrawny, zonked-out, long-haired fellows inside.

This is the "crew" sent by Polecat. I can tell by the look of them that they're not professionals, and even if they were, they don't look physically up to the rigors of cold-weather construction. According to the taller one, who introduces himself as Ned, they're the only crew—partial crew, to be precise—the company has at the moment, the others having quit. Ned has no qualms about bitching about the outfit he's working for. He'd quit, too, if he wasn't so in debt. His sidekick, Randy, parrots the indictment. Oh yeah, don't they know! Polecat's the most disorganized, screwed-up company they've ever worked for. Everything's slow as molasses—schedules, shipments, paychecks. The president's a millionaire, but the company's gone bankrupt twice. Each job they're sent out on is a "lawyer job," that is, a last-minute effort to stave off a lawsuit. But they're here to build my garage, says Ned, hawking a glob of phlegm into a hibernating rosebush. My faith is hardly bolstered.

The last hour or so of daylight gets off to a rocky start. Over the weeks, the holes have partially filled in, and there's ice and water at the bottom. Ned and Randy have brought only one shovel. At the speed they're working, between cigarettes and general exhaustion, they'll never get all twelve holes prepared for the dry-mix concrete footers—their goal for the day. They may not even finish one. I feel I have no choice but to assist them, and thus my wish for hands-on participation comes true. I hand Billy a shovel of mine and get busy with the two-handled digger.

The next day, after the concrete has set overnight, Randy and Ned don't show up until after 11 A.M., wheezing and complaining about the wind off the bay. I help in setting the posts one by one—backfilling, bracing, checking for plumbness. Then we nail kickplates and girts all the way around. As we progress, it's obvious that Randy is more beginner than apprentice. He can't hammer straight, nor can he measure and saw with any accuracy, although Ned assigns him both these jobs and doesn't seem to give a damn when a board comes up inches short, or its nails are half-driven-in and bent over. Randy can't read a spirit level either; it galls me to see some girts so obviously uphill and down. When the jackleg duo takes a break to go to the Chestertown McDonald's, I grab my nail-puller and undo as many of their mistakes as I can. Unfortunately, there's no such tool as a board stretcher.

That afternoon, I help them lift the trusses into place—a job they simply cannot perform alone—and earn my co-workers' ire by insisting that the trusses be spaced and nailed properly. On my own, I add stamped-metal "hurricane" brackets to ensure that the roof system won't lift in a high wind. After the trusses are secured, Ned and Randy are too bushed to continue, so they leave for their motel early.

The next morning, Thursday, they show up a little after ten and seem in better spirits. Ned tells me they've had a night of shooting pool and drinking beer. But a winter storm is rolling in from the midwest, so their plan is to sheath the roof and head out, driving nonstop back to Indiana to see their girlfriends. Their work ethic, due to the time constraint, is just short of feverish now. Ned climbs up into the trusses to set the purlins, I'm the saw-man, and Randy is go-fer. Ned is shaking so much from the cold (he's wearing a thin flannel shirt, cap, and gloves with holes) that he drops tape measure, pencil, cigarettes, everything he tries to hold. A hammer narrowly misses my head and a falling two-by-four knocks Randy to the ground. Nails rain from Ned's frozen fingers. He's saving measurement time on the purlins by not staggering them between trusses the way he should. When he's laying up the roof sheathing, I can see that he's skimping on the nails and H-clips. Moreover, he's not spacing the sheathing right; he's left six inches of nothing—and nothing to nail to—at one gable wing.

Randy uproots brace and batter boards, leaving them on the ground with nail points sticking through. Between saw cuts, I go around clinching the nails because I can't remember when I last had a tetanus shot. I'm half-crazed with lip-buttoned anger. Not only is the level of workmanship appalling, the construction site is downright dangerous. Drink containers and candybar wrappings and cigarette butts litter the mud. Both Randy and Ned seem egregiously pain-prone. Complaining of headaches and indigestion, they pop a variety of acid-stomach nostrums during their too-frequent breaks and blow snot without benefit of handkerchief or sleeve.

When the last sheathing board is nailed at the roof peak, the two of them, as if by prearranged signal, make a dash for the van. From the driver's window, Ned informs me that they'll return, God willing, early next week. As per the contract, I write a check for their services, but I warn Ned not to expect any more money until I've had a chat with the boss. The delays, my legal fees, and my own labor will have to be deducted from the final draw. Ned, gunning the van, says he reckons that's fine with him. Alone, I spend the last hours of sunlight correcting what I can and re-nailing the roof.

The next morning it snows, but there's little accumulation, so I figure I might as well get some construction done on my own. I start putting up sheets of wall siding. The four-by-eight sheets, bowed and cumbersome, aren't the easiest things for one person to work with, but there's a knack to handling them that involves setting them along a temporary rail and nailing them laterally from center to edge. I reach the end of one wall, turn the corner, and begin the next. I don't mind working by myself; it's actually relaxing to take my time and do the job right. Over the weekend, I get all the way around the four walls, and on Monday and Tuesday, I start on the gable ends. On the ladder, the angle measuring is tricky, as is the sawing and the balancing, but I manage okay. Clinging to the rungs, I rehash all the reasons why I shouldn't entrust this phase of the carpentry to anyone but myself. Later, surveying the good results, I'm almost wishing Ned and Randy *won't* reappear.

On Wednesday afternoon, just as I'm starting on the soffit

trim, the van with Indiana plates roars up, and Ned and Randy, accompanied by one of their girlfriends and her baby, climb out. Something in the way they loiter beside the van tells me they haven't come to work. "Gee, I never seen so much water," says the girlfriend, and then, without so much as a by-your-leave, Ned announces that he and Randy have been pulled off the job because *I'm* not being cooperative. They've come to pick up their tools and ladders. Boss's orders. They're heading for a job-site in South Carolina where it's warm.

At this juncture, I confess to playing Br'er Rabbit begging not to be thrown into the briar patch. "Can't you guys stay a little longer and help me shingle the roof?" Like I really want the shingle courses to be wavering all over the place and handfuls of roofing nails caltropping the ground. "It wouldn't take more than a day, the three of us working together." Like I really want to work alongside these idiots and internalize every friggin' thing they do wrong.

"Nope, no can do. Bossman says we gotta leave."

With a faked show of remorse, I hang around while they pack up, mainly to make sure they don't walk off with any of my tools. I have to hand it to Ned and Randy: they're riding the tripartite tiger of inadequate training, poor health, and indispensability. For half-assed work, there'll always be some contractor willing to pay their kind, and pay well. Meanwhile, the girlfriend has been housecleaning the van; in an unconscious gesture of farewell, she pushes her trash out onto the driveway. I'm thankful she'll remain a stranger to the bay—there are too many like her here already. As the van disappears beyond the curve in the road, I sense a great weight lifting from my shoulders. Those shingle bundles will be crushingly heavy, hauling them from pallet to roof by myself, but not as heavy as living with a mis-carpentered eyesore for the rest of my years here.

So I finish the garage on my own. It takes another two weeks of sub-freezing work—especially onerous when the wind-chill dips—and before I'm done, I come down with the flu. Recuperating, I devise all sorts of legal strategems for getting back at Polecat Structures, Inc. Our lawyer judiciously points out the folly of each of them. Legal fees in any lawsuit would be gargantuan, she says, and evidence would be hard to acquire, and even if I won a judgment for a million dollars, I'd never collect. The moral is: never deal with an out-of-state firm. So much for ads at the back of a magazine.

When I'm feeling better, I focus on the positive aspects of the garage-building episode. I've had the opportunity to use tools, among them a chalk line and a four-foot level, that I haven't needed in years. Dollar-wise, I'm no further in the hole than I would have been if I'd begun the project on my own. Above all, I have the satisfaction of knowing that this structure, like all my previous construction projects, is built with care and, as such, built to last.

By early spring, painted and landscaped, the garage looks as if it has always stood there, in harmony with the surroundings, adding a cubic cachet concealing everything on wheels that had previously been parked in what used to be the driveway or on the lawn. Indeed, I feel like exulting, as local poet Geneva "Nena" K. Davis did in the concluding quatrain of her poem, "1976":[4]

> Let's all give thanks to the one above
> Who led us this way,
> To this land of hope and peace and love,
> Tolchester! By the Bay.

chapter
7

Our most frequent visitor on the bluff is a dog. Barely a year old, amber as lager, rambunctious and well fed, it represents a breed of retrievers prized by hunters, and its *itness* testifies to its neutered state, a transformation that occurred not long ago—around the time its puppyhood chronologically ended, although nothing in the way of maturity seems to have replaced it. A more gregarious eunuch I've yet to meet. As dogs go, this one is friendly to a fault, and what's more, in my presence it simply cannot contain itself. It seems to have permanently sized me up as a rompworthy pal.

From afar, I've seen it behave with decorum around its master and mistress, who keep it under control with rebukes and swats—and more recently, a shock collar—but whenever I enter the picture, the dog forgets everything and goes gaga. Jubilantly, it rushes over to me, yelping and leaping, flattering—and almost flattening—me with attention. Other times, it wriggles belly-wise along the ground, head and ears cocked, squealing and squirming, until, springing up, it commences to nip at me, mauling with rough, muddy forepaws. It doesn't intend any harm, so I try not to take its annoying habits personally. An animal behaviorist would call it an exhibition of unconditional love and an invitation to play.

I wish I knew what I did to deserve this treatment. I've tried not to encourage the dog in any way. If anything, I *dis*courage it time and again—like when I'm dressed to go to town, or carrying groceries, or working on a watercolor, or cultivating tender plants. The dog can't appreciate the nuance of fragility. Insistently, it seeks to invade my sphere, as if a change of heart on my part is forthcoming and I'll soon be frolicking one-on-one. At wit's end, I've scolded, hollered, cursed, imitatively barked, and still it comes on like gangbusters. From me, the dog can't take no for an answer. Something about my presence must relax its inhibitions, stir up its molecules. I'm glommed onto as if I were the canine equivalent of catnip—a reason for nuttiness and delirium.

This dog is intelligent enough to know that I don't like what it does, yet it persists in its behavior. It arrives in our yard of its own accord, recharged with affection, assaulting me like a long-lost friend. That this love-fest is habitually one-sided and out of control is incontrovertibly true; nevertheless, I hesitate to dampen the dog's raucous spirit. Although, in my besieged condition, I can hardly be expected to reciprocate love in return, something in me doesn't want to see the dog slink away either. I'd prefer not to get involved, period. But when the creature craves me the way it does, taunting me with comradely love, it's hard to say no. If I attempt to quell its agitation with a firm pat or two, it becomes all the more hyper, at which point I can't help but marvel at its display of energy. As it wheels and lunges in strenuous competition with the laws of gravity, euphoria is evidenced in its narrowed eyes and bare-fanged grin—euphoria of which I am the cause. In such a state, the dog has absolutely no concept of having worn out its welcome. If I were the least unsteady on my feet, I'd be knocked to the ground.

When it is visiting, which is almost daily, our two cats preventatively scatter treeward. I don't think the dog would actually harm them in a nose-to-nose confrontation, but in the order of things, a fleeing feline is the object of a chasing canine, and these cats are too proud to succumb to such pedestrian inevitability. They elect not to be chased. Disdainful of this goofy interloper, they also undoubtedly resent its appropriating what's left in their food bowl, but intuitive good sense makes them withdraw rather than raise their fur. Ever curious, they keep watch, Cheshire-like, from the camouflage of high foliage as the dog sniffs their lingering scents, its telltale irrepressibility furiously signaling from behind.

The ebullient tail is an indicator, I think, of chronic immaturity. No pup anymore, it can't quite take leave of its juvenile obsessions—thanks, perchance, to the neutering. This dog apparently doesn't know the dozing contentedness of lying in the sun or beside a fire; rather, it roams *con brio* until it is called home to be fed, then stuffed into a wire cage for the night. In the freedom of its daily circuit, the dog has no parameters that relate to the exercise of caution. It literally follows its nose anywhere: I've seen it saunter right up to the precipice of the bluff as if it were ready to trot on air. In one place or another, rabbits, squirrels, possums, groundhogs, mice, and robins all announce their tantalizing presence at ground level. Humpy mole tunnels twist along the turf. Spritzable tree trunks abound. The compost pile is an ever-beckoning target for nasal examination, as are buried bones, wild animals' rest areas, and any number of other earthly pungencies of which people remain congenitally unaware. When the dog is conducting its zig-zag inspections, it personifies canineness in its nose-lowered determination, but as soon as its sensory radar zeroes in on me—uh-oh, here we go again.

In me, the dog must sense a kindred spirit, a long-lost buddy on the astral plane. Is it my aftershave, my tone of voice, the fug of my old Eisenhower jacket? Is it my mundane gestural arsenal, different from another person's in ways only a dog can perceive? Sometimes I wonder if, by fluke, I've been reincarnated in the wrong species: I should be—or perhaps I was—somebody's hound.

Beneath my outwardly conformist characteristics, I suppose there's a deeper personality that attracts the dog. I'm not just the quiet neighbor gent puttering about in his yard; I'm also the lover of the cosmos bent on discovering all there is to discover amid phenomena too incredible for words. Perhaps this dog can sense that I also sniff the surroundings, moving from one rapture to the next, and that, metaphorically, I lift my leg as an artist to mark my trail of delight.

Another recurring visitor, mostly nocturnal, is a homeless cat. Unlike the dog, this cat avoids me like the plague. From afar, it eyes me suspiciously, poised to bolt at the slightest provocation. To my credit, I know enough not to advance in its direction, because many years ago, I tried to make a closer acquaintance with a wild kitten, and the result was a painful bite on the hand, followed by an even more painful series of rabies shots. I would expect this hapless creature to bite as well, if cornered. Whatever the neighbor's dog finds attractive about me, this cat evaluates from a distance and steers clear. My only good trait, apparently, is my stewardship of the catfood bowl.

On occasion, when the stray and I accidentally arrive in the vicinity of each other, as when I step outside at night to gaze at the stars, the feline vanishes post haste. By day, through the window, I've seen it slink along the brushy edge of the bluff, a mottled gray loner, shaggy and unkempt, with a scarred, frightened mug and a tail missing chunks of fur. Nightly brawls are this cat's specialty, and by day, in its recuperative mode, it hangs around recessively, as if expecting the worst. Mostly, it is awaiting a turn at the food bowl, which sits on the bottommost step outside the kitchen door. Even when the stray's eyes are invisible in the dark, I know it's out there, biding its time. Since no feline admits to such a thing as a hurried meal, the would-be bowl-finisher has to be patient until our two are sated. Then, checking for danger on all sides, it moves closer until it can settle into a gluttonous crouch. The already-full feasters, mother and son, raise no objection; they're washing themselves nearby and it doesn't occur to them to interfere with the interloper. Our cats are too smart to defend their source of nutrition; what they defend instead is their right to remain indifferent. Inured to even the concept of intrusion, they continue to groom themselves, keeping a watchful eye.

The intrusive part comes much later, after my wife and I have switched off the lights and tucked ourselves into bed. Then, it would appear, the territorial stakes rise significantly. The stray is still hanging around, but the feline chemistry has altered for the worst: the era of live-and-let-live is over. Now it seems that everybody's spoiling for a fight. The two domestics caterwaul malevolently at the stray, which croons back like a rusty siren. Phrases of simultaneous battle cry are terminated with earsplitting—when it's right beneath the window—yowlps, and somewhere in the dark, contact is made, an aurally augmented claw swipe, followed by chasing and scrambling.

The sound of one creature terrifying another is second nature to Nature. With these cats, it's a trio of peaks and valleys; the fray is ripped right into, then a standoff ensues, then another fray, then another standoff during which the harpy serenade wavers at a lower frequency before flaring up into a new episode of terror. The only way I can break it up is to drag myself from bed, navigate to the kitchen, fling open the door, and stamp my feet, hollering at the night. The cats stop then, perhaps because they enjoy witnessing my curious, effete objections. Invisible to me, the stray slinks off even as our own pets appear on the doorstoop, unruffled and affectionate as always, angling for a late-night handout, or at the very least, a pat on the head. Later the caterwauling may recommence, but I'm dreaming too deeply to notice.

The homeless cat's haunting of the premises is a reminder that the verso of any comfortable existence is dependence upon charity. My charitable impulse in this instance is nothing to brag about, but I do admit to putting out a bit more food than our cats can handle. That some creature of the wild gobbles it up doesn't exalt me in any way. I'm making no inroads of friendship, nor am I effecting a conversion to domesticity (the stray is no Eliza Doolittle, moldable, thanks to my effort, into something tame or tractable). The truth is, I'm getting nowhere with that cat, and, to judge by my wee-hour awakenings, the cat's getting nowhere with me. Yet as a visitor, the homeless puss fits into the larger scheme. For all I know, the stray could be supplementing its diet with critters we need fewer of. Even with its nonresident status, it just might be earning its keep.

The herd of deer that routinely drops in along the bluff demands another kind of charity, that of the involuntary sort. The deer have made a habit of nipping flower blooms and buds with a thoroughness that sorely tempts a non-hunter like me to raise a rifle out of season. At first we thought it was only pansies they were after, but it turns out that the list of flowers that whet a deer's palate is a long one, including many delicate annuals and perennials, as well as tougher fare such as sunflowers and hollyhocks. The first spring after we move here, we learn the hard way: from the local garden center, my wife brings home flat after colorful flat, the contents of which she distributes in sundry beds, boxes, and at the bases of trees. Within a day or two, except for the marigolds, almost everything is reduced to unprepossessing stems and leaves—or, in some instances, stems alone.

Though irked, K is undeterred. With experimentation, she discovers some of the blooms that deer eschew, such as begonia, nicotiana, snapdragon, and black-eyed Susan. Early flowering bulbs, as well as irises and day lilies, prove to be unappetizing to the deer's taste buds, too. We soon learn to grow salad greens— lettuce, arugula, cilantro, parsley, and snow peas—in deer-proof fashion, bordering the rows with marigolds. The lady who runs a farm produce stand on the road to Chestertown recommends another effective deterrent: human urine. She apprises us of one of deer hunting's cardinal rules—when in a tree stand, always pee into a bottle, never on the ground. Applying the inverse of that rule to the perimeter of our garden, I can only claim limited success: fresh hoofprints still occasionally show up.

The deer herd, composed of a couple of does and four or five older fawns, can arrive at any hour of the day or night, emerging from the woods on the inland side of the road. Browsing, the timorous tawny ghosts with voracious appetites work their way across the greensward, through the shade trees, right up to the house, repeatedly raising their heads with that big-eared, wide-eyed look of wonderment that belies a sophisticated watchfulness. They're bold, but not in the least assertive. The does' vigilance is mimicked by the fawns as they daintily nibble, ever alert for cues of peril.

Like the herons on the beach that fly away at the slightest awareness of me gazing down at them, the deer are amazingly human-sensitive. Even when I stalk the marauding herd from inside the house, tiptoeing from window to window and incrementally parting the curtains, the deer home in on my presence. Their first reaction is to freeze, thereby allowing many a cammied Nimrod in the field to squeeze off a fatal shot; but not for a second, not even in their momentary inertness, are deer at a loss for an avenue of escape—unless they're dead. Premonitory instinct tells them where to go and how to get there. At the signal of a snort from the lead doe, the herd bounds away, white tails flashing, into the umber recesses of the woods.

K can't say no to a bargain-priced flat of purple petunias, so I help her create yet another flowerbed, this one around the base of a dogwood tree facing the kitchen. It's a substantial project, and when every petunia is set, tamped and watered, we really have something to admire. Then, as Saturday afternoon lethargy sets in, we take a postprandial snooze. By the time we're up and around again, the new bed is bloomless. The stealthy deer have come and gone, leaving the decapitated plants, many of them yanked out of the dirt, as reminders of their discriminating palate. I can't help but see the farcical aspect of our efforts. Instead of gardening, we were catering. We prepared a delectable treat and positioned it in the yard as centerpiece for a banquet. Trouble is, we haven't been paid, not even by a glimpse of our graceful gourmands.

Human visitors don't disturb the flowers, or bother us with crazy displays of affection, or pick fights with our pets. All they do is wax rhapsodic about the bay view. Vociferously—more so, if they're here for the first time—they expand upon the uniqueness of the setting, ooh-ing and ah-ing as if they've been plunked down on heaven's scenic overlook. This kind of reaction always puts K and me in the embarrassing position of not appearing to gloat, because, while we're in full agreement with them on the Chesapeake's allure, we feel the necessity, for modesty's sake, to shrug off the compliments. "Well, yes, we like it here," we lamely reply, eliciting still more superlatives about how relaxed we look and how lucky we are.

Those who know us from the old days see K and me as love-birds come together, after years of B-marriages to other people, in a rugged, dreamy, off-the-beaten-path place. We're likened to pioneering homesteaders or some other impossibly romantic role model: the couple that found happiness at the edge. "How did you ever discover this?" they ask, not expecting our standard answer that a realtor's computer matched our requirements to available listings, much in the manner of a dating service.

But beneath the glowing comments, I can detect skepticism. What all the effusion boils down to, 98 percent of the time, is something I call the Tourist's Distinction: *this is a great place to visit, but not necessarily to live.* The oohs and ahs are another way of saying, subtextually, "You guys must be out of your gourds!"

The fact that my wife and I are, at this stage of things, settled here year-round can be disconcerting to the person who arrives and is peremptorily overcome by the coastal vastness and the grandeur of the elements. The Tourist's Distinction momen-tarily weighs romance against practicality, and comes down firmly on the side of the latter. Why aren't we in a maintenance-free townhouse in a state-of-the-art subdivision, where the living is so much easier? And from the younger fry: "What's there to do around here?" First-time impressionability can be fun—conversation beneath the sassafras, a meal shared, a swim or a walk, an overnight in one of the slant-walled bedroooms upstairs (and choice-of-boxes breakfast the next morning)—but when the hour of departure is nigh, our guests are invariably eager to be on their way. The shorter the sojourn, the better, in most cases. They've had a great time, for which they thank us profusely;

still, there's a longing in their eyes to be returned to a less in-
choate surround. They want to be walled in again. They need urban and suburban rampantness to remind them that they exist.
If, by some miscalculation, they overextend their stay here, they
grow uncomfortable. Just sitting in a chair and staring out to the
water is too mind-consuming, too much like work—and like
work, it gets old after a while. By and by, boats, birds, and breezes
become boring. The visitors are at a loss for more familiar stimulation. Do we have cable or satellite, they ask. They drop hints
that they're ready to go sightseeing, and would we please enumerate some of the historic must-sees in the vicinity. They're
like a train off the tracks, useless and going nowhere, and that's
when, despite the smiles, the sociality can turn sour. It's best to
let them get in their cars and disappear before their smiles do.

We're all visitors in places where we sometimes feel ill at
ease. In a strange locale, our limits of endurance are sure to
be tested; it could be claustrophobia or agoraphobia, or unfamiliar scenery, or bad weather, or bad food; it could be ambient pollution in one form or another—*their* pollution as opposed to
ours (which we've gotten so used to we don't consider pollution
anymore). I used to think that quietude was something almost
everyone wanted eventually—until I found myself with a
mother-in-law who couldn't fall asleep unless her bedside television set was turned *on*. And I can readily see how certain
repetitive stimuli on the waterfront could bug the hell out of
visitors—the concerti of wind and waves, the squawking and
honking and incessant chirruping, the overlayered dronings of
marine propulsion.

So it's understandable why visitors might shrink from this
bay-specific input; it can be, in a word, daunting. Anybody
hooked on passive, electronically provided entertainment might
miss the boat, so to speak. Nothing here unreels itself with
breathless expectation. A typical day develops slowly, its myriad
events cued to seasonal imperatives, and there's a randomness
to be factored in, too. Vectors of bird and insect flight, wakes of
vessels, breeze disruption of boughs—all these, including every

other chance occurrence and juxtaposition, combine in an un-
folding scenario of unpredictability. Beyond the assurance that
the sun and tide will rise and fall, there's no fait accompli—no
plot line, no deepening mystery, no happy, or unhappy, ending.
The day may start with a clear blue sky that turns cumulus by
noon, quilt-like and diffuse by 3 P.M., and stormy by suppertime.
The breeze, formerly caressing, now batters leaf and limb. Later,
the sun may set in glorious technicolor above the Western
Shore, or it may go into hiding behind a purple cloud bank, casting the bay in a drab limbo twilight that questions its very existence as an aqueous medium.

In my observation, most of our visitors shut down their senses
long before any of this can sink in. Typically, they don't come
here seeking a meditative experience, but rather to socialize, and
when that saturation point is reached, they either search for
something else in the way of conversation, or announce their
imminent departure. Keeping guests happy means turning away
from quiet reflection, which is fine with me, for I often meditate
too long and can use the break.

No, I don't object to guests. After a long stretch by ourselves,
my wife and I are both delighted when company arrives. Furthermore, I like to think that I'm a good host: I listen, I draw—
not drown—people out, I mind read. I know, for example, when a
guest's overriding concern is the procurement of the next drink,
the next go-round of the hors-d'oeuvres platter. I give ear to the
recounting of visitors' recent mini-vacations in four-star resorts,
their prowess at trading in a car that is ten years younger than
mine, their ongoing battle with the contractor who is redoing
their kitchen. I excuse them when they need to check their
voicemail messages, or when their beepers suddenly ensnare
their attention as I'm pointing my finger at a passing bald eagle.

When visitors take nothing away from here other than their
superficial impressions, I don't feel slighted in the least. Instead,
I'm relieved that they haven't fallen so in love with the place
that they're considering moving next door. As it turns out, there
is a house for sale next door, just past the wooded lot to the

south of us, and while it's nothing to write home about—a one-and-a-half story bungalow with a screened-in porch—it has a certain recherché appeal. Unlived in, it has been on the market for almost two years; and like every other waterfront listing around here, it is overpriced. Still, plenty of potential buyers have been coming by to take a look.

My wife and I would like to see it sold, not only because it's a prime target for vandalism, but also because trespassers have been using its bluff-side stairway to get down to our beach. To this end, I confess to acting as a salesman without portfolio. The first person I tried to get interested in the bungalow was the man who delivered the roof trusses for the garage. Maybe because he hailed from Indiana, he seemed inordinatly smitten by the watery locale (he went on and on about the length of the Bay Bridge). Seemingly cooperative and friendly, he fulfilled the foremost requirement of a potential neighbor. In my rap to him, I stressed the bungalow's apparent sturdiness and the fact that its roof was sound. I strongly urged him to consider moving east, where opportunities in the construction trade were many, and where he could fish, day in and day out, from his very own pier. In retrospect, I realize I was wasting my breath, because, in the end, my fervent wish was that I neither see nor hear from him or his company again. Fortunately, my wish was granted.

My second "client" was the tree surgeon who removed the colossal, half-dead Kentucky coffee tree that stood in the front yard, dangerously shedding limbs on the new garage. This young fellow, soon to be married, told me he was looking for a place to live, so I immediately sized him up as a worthy candidate. I pointed out the intimacy of the bungalow's setting, the variety of shrubbery and ornamental trees surrounding it that would benefit from his pruning saw. He may indeed have called the agent, but nothing came of it. My guess is that the price discouraged him, but it could also have been that he and his bride-to-be were planning on having a large family.

The third time I donned the guise of self-appointed realtor was on a beautiful Saturday morning in early June when I happened to be swimming, for the first time that season, about a hundred and fifty yards offshore. Suddenly I was aware of cries from the bluff in the vicinity of the bungalow: "Are you all right out there? Are you sure you're all right?"

I could see two tiny figures waving at me, so I rotated until my feet touched bottom, stood up in the chest-high water and waved back at them, furnishing the picture worth a thousand words. Satisfied, the couple proceeded to engage me in a conversation, which, at that distance, consisted of yells back and forth. Cupping their hands, they inquired about the bungalow, asking all the usual questions, while I, three-quarters submerged, yelled back. They wanted details: what kind of heat, what kind of hot water, was it air-conditioned? I told them that I had never actually been in the house, but I had looked in the windows. No, I wasn't aware of its exact age, nor did I know what the property taxes were, although I could furnish educated guesses.

Judged by their queries and their earnestness (to the point of hoarseness), these people seemed like serious buyers. I poured it on about what an upstanding community this was, mentioning a snippet or two about its history. I praised the new sewer line, the roads, the negligible incidence of crime, the fresh northwesterly wind, the birdwatching, the boating, the swimming. I vouched for the smoothness of the sandy bottom on which I stood. My panegyric could have gone on and on, but I was feeling a bit chilled and had to excuse myself to swim back to the beach. But I told them to walk on over to our house in fifteen minutes or so if they had more questions. I never saw them again. I got to thinking that maybe I had told them too much, or sounded too eager, or tried too hard, or committed some faux pas that a more subtle salesperson would have avoided. But I had to work fast to ward off the shivers. Whatever I did wrong, I lost no commission.

The last person I exerted my persuasiveness on was a woman from Rock Hall in search of a small dwelling for her aged mother. I made her acquaintance at the mailboxes across the street from the bungalow. Having toured the property without benefit of a realtor, she had a number of pressing questions. The first thing she wanted to know was whether the inexorable rise in sea level made a bayfront home a bad investment. I told her it depended on how long her mother might live. At the current rate of one to three feet a century, the forty-foot bluff would be getting soggy around the time her mother was slightly older than Methuselah. But what, she asked, about shoreline erosion? Wasn't the bluff—and the houses thereon—in danger of washing away long before that? I admitted that she had a point: in all likelihood, her descendants would have neither the dough nor the desire to spring for thousands upon thousands of cubic yards of rip-rap. But not to worry—nobody else would either. No, the bluff would not outlast Time, and at some juncture down the line, there would be a general write-off of most waterfront property in conjunction with a mass societal exodus toward the higher altitudes of the heartland.

But then I corrected myself. I told her there would always be a select number of foolhardy folk who would insist on living at the water's edge. These people would retreat and retreat, but they'd never be willing to forsake their symbiotic relationship with the coastline. In their minds, a water vista would always be equated with freedom. They'd rather live in hurricane-exposed shacks than earthquake-proof highrises. It wouldn't matter how crowded and jumbled the land behind them got; they'd stake their fortunes on the crumbling cusp.

Through the grapevine several weeks later, I heard that the woman decided to purchase a small bayfront home south of here in the vicinity of the marina. She must have liked my ideas, but she may not have thought it suitable for her mother to dwell next door to a mailbox philosopher. I decided it was time to keep my mouth shut and let the bungalow sell itself. So far it hasn't.

chapter
8

Something—I suspect it's the clarity of the coastal light—makes me start painting again. I haven't picked up a watercolor brush in several years, having every excuse in the world not to paint, and, like a fool, making good on each one. Now I'm glad to have run out of excuses; I've told myself, it's either get back into painting or hang it up forever.

My subject, the bayside, is right under my nose. Carrying my painting kit and a folding chair to shady locations alongside the house, under the trees and taller bushes, by the outbuildings, or on the fishing deck and beach in the morning shadow of the bluff, I stalk inspiring views. I choose a spot, plunk myself down in the chair, and arrange my things: paintboxes, watercolor block, water jar, brushes, pencil, gum eraser, paring knife, bug repellent. Then I sit very still and stare. Watching the bay for the purpose of creating art is a skill in itself. Aesthetic decisions need to be arrived at. What, precisely, should my rectangle of inquiry frame, and where should I place its horizon line, and which tonal pallette should I utilize? Sitting and, to all outward appearances, doing nothing, I'm formulating a plan of attack, reviewing the options before committing my lightly penciled outlines to paper. After sketching in what I want to represent, I'm bolder with my color daubs. The secret is to work up to full-tilt inspiration gradually, taking care not to overlook anything that could contribute to the painting's success.

It's new for me to be limiting my visual inquiry to three basic ingredients: land, water, and sky. In my earlier days as a painter, I would have dismissed this kind of subject matter as being simpleminded. I was more concerned with painting the *Sturm und Drang* of my emotions—those fleeting, riotously hued intangibles that needed, I then believed, fleshing out in paint to prove to the world that I had artistic talent. Now, taking up the brush again, the images in my head pale in comparison with what's in front of my eyes. Understandably, I've succumbed to the Chesapeake's atmospheric lucidity, which bears a similarity to that of Venice and the Netherlands—a quality that tells me to celebrate the visible, not the imaginary.

I've also learned that painting a bayscape is no piece of cake. Plenty of reduction and extrapolation in both detail and impression is called for. If my goal is to interpret nature, not to ape it, the finished product will illustrate but a fraction of the fullness. From the smorgasbord that's visually gorged upon, I must choose carefully, for less is more when it comes to controlling a watercolor. Selectivity is the key: knowing what to put in and what to leave out. Moreover, I pride myself on not being the kind of artist who resorts to overly facile tricks of technique as taught in myriad watercolor classes by charlatans who thrive on suffocating the walls of the world with bad art.

Scrutinizing a view to be painted, my eyes discern all manner of input that begs for inclusion, but my brush hand, taking orders from my brain, eliminates most of it. I'm searching for essence, not persiflage. It's my artistic duty to edit out anything that overloads the painted statement. As a rule, my bayscapes are neither peopled, animaled, nor birded, and only rarely do I throw in a boat.

Another reason I prefer an uncomplicated composition is that I work small now, whereas in the past I refused to be encumbered by size restrictions. As one of those MFA-clad tyros specializing in a signature postmodern style, I used to believe that visual impact had mostly to do with the physical size of the painting. Like so many other emerging artists, I purported to be in the vanguard (the vanguard of what?—there were so many vanguards).

Nowadays, my grandiose aspirations are over, kaput. As far as painting goes, I'm no longer trying to impress the gods—or become one myself. Taking a chunk of the normal field of vision, framing it in my mind's eye, then committing it to the rectangle of paper (and later, in the studio, to stretched canvas, also small) is all I set out to accomplish. What interests me is the pleasurable aspect of visual creativity, the sheer joy of being outdoors and exercising my perception. I can, for instance, choose a foreground that includes a portion of the bluff-edge, behind which the receding plane of water meets the horizon line of the Western Shore, and above that, a remarkable sky. The variations and permutations are limitless. I can work with each of the three compositional elements, experiment with them before I tie them all together, and forfeit my ego in the process.

Then, when I use these watercolor studies as the basis for acrylics on canvas in the studio, I have a head start. Working indoors, I can layer up the paint, enhancing both the color and texture of the surface on which I build. Unlike my *modus artis* as a watercolorist, I am slow to finish an acrylic. Unresolved paintings, propped here and there, clutter the work space, awaiting renewed inspiration. A definitive version usually doesn't announce itself until weeks or months afterward, when I've exhausted nearly all my ideas and am frustrated to the point of scraping and re-gessoing the unsatisfying impasto—in other words, starting over—when all of a sudden I stand back and exclaim, "Wow, I just nailed it . . . I think!"

If I didn't have plenty of tints to choose from, and the patience to mix them, I might run into trouble. Primarily, the bay is Prussian blue, but it can also be pale indigo, or Payne's gray, or even purple lake leaning toward lavender, with gradations in between, depending on how the breezes interact with the light, the time of day, the temperature and the humidity. The sky, fundamentally a Cerulean hue, runs the gamut from rose madder to yellow ochre to dioxazine violet, with ultramarine and cadmium orange and mauve kicking in at sunset. As for the bluff's vegetation, emerald, Viridian, sap, and Hooker's greens vie for dominance between gamboge highlights and sepia shadows.

Although I start out with a rational plan, the overlays of paint quickly assume an intelligence of their own. Furiously, the brush struggles to keep abreast of the darting eye. Try this, now try that, and that, and that. Stop, no, go, get busy in another quadrant (see how easy it is?), now come back and resolve this mess over here, that's better. From the sable tips, darks and lights are laid side by side, giving the illusion of definition and volume. A loaded brush is neither weapon nor tool, but an extension of Will; in the act of wielding it, I'm obliterating and creating at the same time—playing Old Testament God, you might say—and my whole being is utterly absorbed in a jabbing, intuitive rhythm. Whatever else I could or should be doing is on hold. The painting's my priority, my purpose, my life. I've literally walked right into its rectangle.

A typical painting session, indoors or outdoors, lasts only an hour or two, three at most. When my creative gas tank reaches empty, I know that no matter what I do, the painting can't be improved. Finished or not, it is placed on one of several easels to be studied at leisure. For me, this is painting, too, sitting ten feet away in my favorite armchair, mulling over what I should change and what I should leave alone. My chief criterion for evaluation is whether I've taken an instant liking to the immediate results. There's no wait-and-see attitude at this point, no pondering. Is there an overall harmony in the composition, is the paint used effectively? I'm trying to create something that'll leapfrog the ordinary, something that'll add one and one and come up with three, and at this juncture, only I can provide the critique. Resolution is always something to marvel at—a miracle, really, of the mind's satisfaction. What I'm striving for is the same thing every other artist strives for: to make the painting come out right.

Veracity, verisimilitude—these I try to incorporate in my work without resorting to photographic realism. I thank God every day that I haven't succumbed to those garden-variety inspirations of so many Eastern Shore painters whose workboats, seagulls, rustic docks, waving grasses, and lighthouses fairly teem with mawkish sentiment. With steadfastness, I have fought every tendency to make my art look as though it could hang comfortably beside carved wooden decoys, or fishnet, or brass ships' clocks, or shell arrangements. I want these bayscapes of mine to be easy to understand, but I also want them to be transcendent. I'm not just demonstrating that the edge of the bay is an engaging place to live and paint. My ultimate aim is to record beauty and, having done so, pass it along.

But who do I pass it along to? Since moving here, I've pretty much been painting in a vacuum. Finished bayscapes are starting to pile up in the studio, crowding out the precious, limited work space. Choosing what I consider the cream of the lot, I strip-frame seven canvases with lattice, affixing screweyes and braided wire to the backs. Then, I select eight watercolors for matting under glass at a frame shop. My plan is to have the paintings ready to show when the world is ready for them.

But when will that happen? As far as exhibition spaces go, there's only one private gallery in Chestertown, and it's crammed with slick crafts and collector's prints, with definitely no room for a newcomer. Washington College is committed to its own art program, in which student shows are given top priority. A downtown bank does monthly exhibits in an alcove leading to the vault, but there's a two-year waiting list. Kent County has a state-funded arts council that rents a suite of rooms in a run-down building off High Street, but nobody but nobody ever walks inside. Operating a "vanity" gallery appears to be my only other option, and that, financially speaking, is out of the question.

I am heartened, therefore, when a retired neighbor, soliciting door-to-door for memberships in the Tolchester Community Association, notices a couple of the paintings hanging in our living room and mentions that I'd be welcome to show my work at the community hall during the annual spring festival on an upcoming Saturday from nine to one. Other arts and crafts people will be exhibiting as well (he names several I haven't yet met), and since he's on the steering committee, he can reserve four free-standing wire-mesh panels for my display, plus a folding chair to sit on. Also, somebody will be in the hall to keep an eye on things in case I'm gone and a buyer walks in—which he can't guarantee, he says, "but, hey, you never know."

"Okay, let's give it a try," I tell him. I'm not overly optimistic, but I've got a framing bill to pay. It sounds like worthwhile first-time exposure—something low-key, something to hit the local art lovers right between the eyes.

And so, at 8:45 on the appointed morn, I transport all fifteen show-ready paintings the few blocks to Montgomery Avenue. Outside the cinderblock hall, on sawbuck-and-plyboard tables, used household items are being given one more lease on life in the twenty-five-to-fifty-cent range. Only a few coffee-steadied souls have bothered to show up. Disinterestedly, they paw through the wares. Nobody seems to have the slightest curiosity about what's going on inside, where I discover, much to my exasperation, that the other exhibitors have set up and gone, leaving no space for me. The woven wreaths, painted crab basket slats, molded plaster figurines, stocking dolls, Christmas baubles, shellscapes, wind chimes, and mailbox appliqués must all have been carted in the day before. Everything has a price tag (between $1.50 and $17.50), but it's already clear that little, if any, of it is going to sell—nobody else is around and the lights haven't been turned on.

But I'm not complaining (there's no one to complain to); I've come to set up an exhibit. Surveying the unpromising scene, I notice a couple of extra panels propped in a dark corner. I calculate how I might be able to scrunch up one whole wall of panels in order to accommodate the unused ones for my own purposes. Gingerly—"You break it, you buy it," read strategically placed index cards—I compress the linear exhibit into an accordion pattern. There, perfect! I arrange the empty panels at one end beside the door and proceed to hang, or rather stagger, my artwork in a vertical mosaic. When I'm done, there's barely a square inch of exposed mesh. I'm reluctant to mention publicly what I think the paintings are worth, so I write "Price on Request" on a business card, which I tape to the center of the display.

My artwork is patently out of place in this sea of homemakers' craft. Here are fifteen painted views of the actual bluff on which our fair community stands, while surrounding them are tables and panels overflowing with wares derived from do-it-yourself pages of magazines found in the checkout lines of any supermarket. It's the old standoff: art versus kitsch. Uncomfortable in this milieu, I'm ready to beat a hasty retreat, but, on second thought, I decide to stick around for a while. Surely, somebody will come in and offer some positive feedback, *somebody* will recognize the effort and originality that has gone into these depictions. I force myself to sit there for an hour and a half, during which one or two people actually do walk in and contemplate my work—and even compliment me on it—but as soon as we start talking, it turns out that they're exhibitors, too, and so I feel obliged to comment appreciatively on their creations.

Eventually, I drive home, filled with frustration at having wasted the better part of the morning. K is out working in the yard, so I join her. The therapeutic effect of gardening is well documented—chiefly, I suspect, because it induces forgetfulness on the part of the gardener. When we take a break for lunch, I realize that the exhibit has completely slipped my mind. It's quarter to one; I hop in the car and drive back to the community hall, but the door is locked and nobody's around. Outside, all the tables are gone—it's as if the yard sale had never occurred. Frantically, I rush home to phone the fellow who got me involved in the first place, but his wife says he's taking a nap. Untold calls later, I track down the presiding official of the community association. She tells me to come directly over to her house, which I do. Hesitantly, she loans me her ring of keys (she must be still smarting from the bingo box theft), and I drive back to the community hall, unlock the door, retrieve the paintings, lock the place up, return the keys, and schlep the artwork homeward. Needless to say, nobody has requested the price of any painting during or since that day's fiasco.

The temptation is strong, but I refuse to become an artistic anchorite. A week or so later, when a brochure for the Chestertown Arts League's annual juried show arrives in the mail, I'm willing to give local exposure another try. From the fifteen paintings that were so temerariously ignored, I select two that I consider to be among my very finest, an acrylic and a watercolor, the former a view of the bluff looking across to Pooles Island and the latter a view looking southward. To the backs of each, I tape the required information cards, with name, address, price, phone number, and insurance value. At the bottom of each card are two blank boxes for acceptance or rejection, one of which will be checked at the moment of truth, the moment I'm paying fifteen dollars per painting for, but by entering work in two media categories, I figure that I'm improving my chances of getting in by 50 percent.

This is the first juried show I've entered in a very long time, and, although it's smaller and more locally oriented than the ones in which I used to participate during my years as an abstractionist, I'm not getting my hopes up. I know nothing about the Arts League, save that it charters buses two or three times a year to the museums of Washington, D.C., and New York City. And I know nothing about the juror's taste in art; the brochure only states that he lives in Centreville and is "a recognized expert" in his field, as well as an author of a "how-to book on painting." With credentials so vague, the least can be inferred; he may be a retired sign painter with a desktop publication, for all I know. I don't mean to pre-judge him, but I have my suspicions and am expecting the worst. I've submitted work to dozens of juried shows and never had much luck. Nine times out of ten, the juror had an ax to grind and it didn't coincide with my own, so nine times out of ten, my work was rejected.

Imagine my excitement, then, when I hear that both paintings have been accepted, and not only that, the acrylic has won third prize in its category. Maybe there exists an enlightened art community in Kent County after all! My wife is tickled; she's telling me that this is a good omen, that things'll break open for me as an Eastern Shore painter, that I needn't worry about being ignored much longer. Third prize! That's better than honorable mention—there'll be a cash award. And it must be a fairly large exhibit, considering that not one, but two Svensons are to be included. To everybody she sees, she brags about my good fortune, and I feel so splendid about myself that I paint with renewed vigor, slathering bolder colors, prodding line and form.

On the afternoon of the show's opening, which is in the foyer of the auditorium at Washington College, K and I arrive early, dressed up and eager to bask in the limelight. With plenty of wine and food, there's a loose egalitarian ambience to the affair, and the jumble of artwork on display is brightly spotlit—a little of everything, some not bad, most not good, which is about what to expect in a regional show of this nature. Taking us aside, one of the docents explains that not a single work has been rejected. Now *that's* something to say in favor of the juror of renown— he's cobbled together a win-win event, making everybody happy. And hanging on the second floor, right in the middle of the lineup, is my acrylic bayscape, blushing beneath its yellow third-place ribbon.

But we're having trouble locating the watercolor. Between trips to the dwindling snack and beverage stockpile, K and I scan the walls thrice over. There are views of boats and birds and barns and backyards and backsides, but *View South Along Mitchell's Bluff* is nowhere in the mix. Perplexed, I ask the docent where we might find it.

"Oh, then this must be yours," she says, extracting the framed watercolor from beneath a table. My heart is both warmed and crushed to see the painting again; warmed to be reminded, at a month's remove, of how decent a watercolor it is, and crushed to realize that it has been deliberately left out of the exhibition.

"But you told me, not fifteen minutes ago, that everything was accepted . . ."

"Everything *was* accepted, but not quite everything is hanging," she says. "We had to work with the space constraints."

"Well, that's a pretty raw deal for some of the artists . . ."

"We realize that and we're sorry," she interrupts, "but the juror had the final say in the hanging process."

I'm truly humiliated. I want to march right up to the probable ex–sign painter, who's holding forth—in plaid jacket and silk ascot, wineglass in hand—in a circle of sycophants, and ask what he found wrong with my work. It's no exaggeration to say that the watercolor is as good or better than any of this stuff, including my own acrylic. I want to rescue the little painting from oblivion and personally exchange it with some inferior creation in a prominent spot, and in the process, make a hero of myself and a fool of him. But, a victim of well-bred manners, I only stand there simmering.

Meanwhile, a janissary of the Arts League is calling for everyone's attention for the presentation of the cash awards. Her list of things to say is a long one, including debts of gratitude to the juror for his cogent and critical eye, to her colleagues for helping to hang the show, to the college for donating the exhibition space, and to the artists for their participation. This is the League's biggest exhibition ever, she says, and, in her opinion, the best. Then she apologizes that cash will only be awarded for first and second prizes this year, due to the increased overhead.

That last item really ticks me off. There'll be no recouping, not even partially, my entry fee. But insult is added to injury when she announces the prizes by category. *No second prize was awarded in acrylics.* There's a first prize, worth fifty dollars, then my third, worth nothing. What a lousy way to trim the budget! For some reason, the juror has sent me an unmistakable message: the watercolor sucks, the acrylic isn't much better. Is it because I'm a newcomer and haven't paid my dues? Is it because he's taken a disliking to my no-frills subject matter? Is it because his own tight-assed realism and my loose brushwork are antipodes apart? (A gilt-framed duck-huntingscape with his signature sits on an easel in the entranceway.) I could throttle him for the impertinence. He doesn't even know me, but I already know him too well—he's the one being treated like some visiting royalty. I want to take a poke at his eminence for singling me out for rejection and cutting me off from the prize money. It takes strenuous effort to keep my wrath in check. The only sweet note to the whole sour affair has been the comestibles. Stung, I'm also sated—not to mention a little tipsy from the chardonnay—and this aids me in saving face when the time comes for my wife and me to leave. Head high, I walk through the crowd and out the door, the watercolor tucked under my arm.

But during the following weeks, my confidence as an artist slips to an all-time low. I'm not inspired to paint anymore, and I'm wondering if my decision to give up nonrepresentational art was ill-considered. I'm thinking that maybe I've bitten off more than I can chew—maybe I *am* no good at painting what I see. Perhaps the bluff and the bay are just too difficult to portray, especially since I haven't been resorting to the standard props that would "sell" them. One of the benefits of painting what's inside your head is that nobody can criticize you for what you've left out.

Then I remind myself that the view from the bluff really is inside my head. I've lived here long enough to have internalized its every nuance. I'm not just painting like a tourist or a technician, cranking out a what-you-see-is-what-you-get rendition. I've become so familiar with the proportions and textures and atmospherics that I'm painting scenes that aren't scenes, but rather states of mind. The painter and etcher James Abbott McNeil Whistler (1834–1903) referred to his compositions as symphonies, harmonies, and nocturnes. He understood that literal depictions—and literal descriptions—didn't do justice to his lyrical representations. Quite possibly, I've gotten myself into the same bind: although I'm depicting what's in front of my eyes, my brushwork seems to be expressing an altogether different reality. Not to worry, I tell myself; the old abstractionist tendencies haven't entirely died out. I'm painting what I see, but, until I paint it, nobody else is seeing it quite the way I am.

Gradually, I wean myself from thoughts of artistic failure, and when my confidence is restored, I go back to a regular painting schedule. It may sound corny, but I'm truly contented when I paint. At the close of the month-long show, I retrieve the acrylic and its yellow ribbon, and think no more about it. Next year, I may enter again, or maybe I'll wait a few years, or maybe I'll tie the yellow ribbon 'round the old oak tree. Time is always on the side of an artist's reputation (consider Van Gogh, who wasn't remunerated for a single work in his lifetime). I have been remunerated in the past, and will be again. And anyway, here on the bay, it always feels as if life is just getting started.

I've come to the conclusion that acceptance of my paintings has more to do with the cosmic throw of the dice than with anything else, and at this stage of the game, I truly speak from years of experience. A better day is, as ever, on the horizon. An acquaintance tells me that Rock Hall, interestingly enough, is becoming the new local mecca for art. A husband-and-wife team from Philadelphia has been rehabilitating moribund commercial real estate at the sleepy harbor town's center. They're a savvy couple, these two; already there's a café, a bookstore, a toy store, numerous boutiques—and the customers are coming. As new businesses are launched, art and craft consignment is encouraged. The opportunity to exhibit is too good to pass up.

With my carload of paintings, I drive the five miles to the formerly provincial outpost. I've always had a good feeling about Rock Hall; I like its unabashed slogan, "Nice People Live Here," and I also like the fact that K and I can go dancing on a Saturday night to a live band on an open deck with no cover charge at Waterman's Restaurant. Also, the road from Tolchester to Rock Hall is one of the pleasanter short drives in Kent County, with sparse traffic and no roadside advertising of any kind. What the future holds for this unspoiled corner of the small county is sometimes fearsome to contemplate. Forests and cornfields are already hard against development sites when the speed limit drops to 25 mph on the outskirts of town.

I find the Philadelphia husband behind a parking lot, not far from his black Mercedes. He's scraping old paint off the clapboard siding of one of their buildings (this one houses a gourmet cookware shop, a doll gallery, and an architect's office). For a part-time Rock Hall dweller, he's a certifiably nice person; he doesn't mind the interruption, and he's willing to look at the paintings on the spot. I prop them in the dusty gravel—a mini-exhibition along rocker panel and wheel wells. He makes a snap decision to take two of the watercolors, his idea being to place them either in the bookstore adjacent to the café, or in a display window of a rental property across the street. As he describes it, he and his wife have created a consignment gallery without walls. Next year he's thinking about opening a real gallery, for which he'd need a lot more of my paintings, he says, but for now, he'd better start with just the two.

His 30 percent commission on sales doesn't faze me, nor do I care how or where he hangs the artwork (for the time being, he'll store the paintings under the cash register desk at the bookstore). He's a go-getter, that's for sure; he drives a fancy car, but he's not afraid to get his hands dirty. I'll trust his judgment and await the check. We conclude our arrangement with a handshake, and I drive home fully convinced that I'm on the threshold of a lucrative venture. But three weeks later, having heard nary a word— nor received anything resembling a check—I drive back to Rock Hall to assess the situation. Walking into the bookstore, I notice that the paintings haven't been moved from where he left them. The clerk professes to know nothing about it, and the boss is conveniently out of town.

Fine, I'll go to the boss of the boss, and so I carry the watercolors over to the café, which is run by the Philadelphia wife. Apologizing for her husband's well-meant but scattered attention ("He's usually doing ten things at once"), she suggests that the paintings be placed on display in the café, which gets the lion's share of the walk-in trade. Something in her unflinching admission convinces me. I let her hang the watercolors, plus two others from the car, on a wall right beside a picture window facing the street. The four paintings look terrific together, and what's more, they can be viewed from the terrace patio as well as from the sidewalk.

In subsequent trips to Rock Hall, I discover that my artwork can also be seen from the car window if I drive by slowly enough and take my eyes off the road just before the blinking light. I wish I didn't see the watercolors at all, because that would mean they had sold. Month after month I prowl past, and all four paintings remain.

chapter

9

In 1943, at the apex of Tolchester Park's spindly roller coaster known as Whirl-Pool Dips, a girl fell out of the gondola.

"She came out of there with arms spread, as quiet as a flying squirrel," says Wilson Ward, a witness. Mr. Ward was in a position to see everything; he was the engineer straddling the miniature steam engine, Jumbo, which pulled trainloads of Brobdingnagian excursionists along the so-called Tolchester Railroad. As he and his passengers traversed the narrow-gauge track that wound along the tree-lined park, through a wooden tunnel resembling an elongated garage, and back to the starting point, a quarter-scale replica of a wide-eaved station, he was awestruck by the sight of the falling girl.

"She landed on top of a tool house, on the only rotten board," he relates. The miraculously cushioned impact knocked the wind out of her, but the girl was quickly resuscitated, with no injuries other than a broken wrist and some missing teeth.

Mr. Ward, a Piney Neck oysterman by trade who donned his engineer's cap and coveralls to supplement his income during the off season, would ultimately serve as the amusement park's last superintendent. He had begun summer work there as a young man in 1922. His part-time career ended when the park closed its gates exactly forty years later.

It is late March, 1965, three years after his retirement, and Mr. Ward is touring the abandoned grounds with R. Hurtt Deringer, news editor of the *Chester River Press*, and I am scanning, thirty-odd years in the future, the yellowed, creased page of newsprint with photographs that had been preserved, along with others in a manila file folder labeled "Tolchester Clippings," by a neighbor's deceased mother. Mr. Ward goes on to recount, to the best of his recollection, that during his tenure at the amusement park only one other person parted ways with a roller-coaster seat, and that was a drunk who fell off the back of the gondola but hung on to the finish, abrading only his shoes.

The five photographs on the brittle page, all taken by Mr. Deringer (who I wish had had space in the layout to include one of old Mr. Ward himself), illustrate the ravages incurred during the park's three closed seasons. Ben Day dots conjur up the limpid tail end of winter: the sky is the newsprint itself, and elsewhere, reflection and shadow conspire to accentuate the starkness of the neglected, deteriorating scene. Behind gone-to-seed grass, the park's structures appear naked, as if stripped of the veneer—of purpose, of upkeep—that clothed them for the masses who once swarmed around and through their pleasure portals. Still-sound roofs and load-bearing posts defy the elements, except that now it's a useless burden, as irrelevant as the lintels of Stonehenge. Utility poles, wires sagging, support old-fashioned enamel-on-steel light reflectors shaped like washing machine agitators. Three years ago, the electricity was turned off. Today, the world is ignoring these ghosts of former amusements. Spring is on its way, but not a single ticket will be sold.

As Mr. Ward walks with the reporter/photographer through what's left of the park in 1965, I'm following along, via the five pictures, as if I'm there too. At the top of the page is the twin-towered pavilion of vaguely Italianate design that stands at the foot of the bluff, closest to the steamboat pier. It's one of the few structures that wasn't hidden by trees in summertime. Day excursionists en route from the far side of the bay remember it as the park's landmark, its flag-topped towers visible nearly ten miles away. In the pavilion's heyday, a snack bar and restaurant operated beneath the first-floor arches, and on the second floor, behind ornate balustrades, was a dance hall. Now the pavilion is a defunct, boarded-up firetrap with a faded sign on one shingled column advertising steamed crabs and beer. Prior to the park's hardscrabble penultimate decade, alcoholic beverages were expressly forbidden (and forbidden on the excursion vessels from Baltimore as well)— a policy that distinguished Tolchester from other amusement parks and endeared it to boatloads of Sunday School picnickers.

The next photograph, counterclockwise, shows the hangar-like structure that once held the fun house and rifle range. Rebuilt after a fire damaged its predecessor in 1952, it also contained, during various seasons, a pool hall, a penny arcade, and a frozen dessert counter called "Creamy Whip." The photograph below includes the railroad station (the scale confirmed by a seemingly oversize bench) and, adjacent to it, an open-sided arc-roofed building with "Skooter" emblazoned across its gable. Here were the solo-seat bumper cars—each powered by a pole scraping along the electrically energized chickenwire ceiling— that collided cartoonishly on the bare metal floor.

At the lower left of the page is an interior shot of the now-empty carousel, with a hand-lettered sign spelling "gninraw," betraying the photograph's mirror-image printing. The capacious shuttered building, 240 feet in circumference, is just a shell. Strewn over its formerly oiled floorboards is litter—paper or rocks or something else not quite distinguishable. To the far side, a ticket booth sits in shadow, although the circular bank of clerestory windows blazes with daylight. Mr. Ward relates that the merry-go-round was brought to the park in 1917, run by steam at first, then converted to gasoline engine in 1921. Its wooden animals and birds, hand-carved and painted in Germany, were finished so exquisitely that not a single seam could be found. Tolchester's previous carousel, installed in the 1880s, was powered by donkey; the very first one, dating back to the park's origins in 1877, consisted of six small winged horses turned by a hand crank.

Finally, there is a photograph of the Whirl-Pool Dips, a skeleton of a skeleton, a roller coaster on the verge of collapse. One formerly elevated section of track has fallen against the uprights, contrasting with the upward-thrusting limbs of trees behind. The more closely I examine the photograph, the more I perceive structural fragility; quite possibly, the whole thing will fall into a heap of sticks on its own. But according to Mr. Ward, the roller coaster *always* had a reputation for ricketiness, even though— with the exception of the aforementioned incidents—it had an excellent safety record. Originally constructed around 1912, it incorporated an enclosed water-trough braking area at the end of its ride, hence the "pool" dips. In the '40s, part of the structure caught fire and underwent substantial repairs. There was an earlier roller coaster, too, called "Thriller," colloquially known as "Switchback" or "Swishback," that needed a brakeman at its far turn to decelerate through a long, spooky tunnel.

The subjects of these photographs will stand, more or less, for a few more years (photographs in the *Kent County News* taken in August, 1969, attest to the further encroachment of weeds and multiflora as soffits disintegrate and siding gapes) before being torn down. For $75,000, the property has been acquired at auction by its mortgage holders; later, it will be purchased by a local entrepreneur named Bramble, who intends to establish a marina and a residential subdivision. Deconstructing an amusement park of Tolchester's size is no small task: after selling off all salvageable gear, the bulldozing, burning, and burying will take months. Few members of the local populace have raised objections on grounds of either history or sentiment; most feel that the past can't be revisited, much less resurrected. The concluding paragraphs of before-and-after newspaper articles reflect the tenor of public opinion:

> Now Tolchester Park is a rotting, decaying ruin, with only the land, its ravines and trees, salvageable for future use. But of this we are sure: whatever Dave Bramble has in mind for the use of Tolchester Park will not be to desecrate or demean it. In fact, we believe it's the other way around. . . .
> *Kent County News*, August 27, 1969

> The whole area has been graded, much of it black-topped, and the sides have been bulkheaded and scores of slips have been built for boat dockage. . . .

As for the old park itself, all of the buildings and rides have been razed, good hard-surfaced roads wind in and out through the groves of trees and up and down ravines once crossed by wooden bridges . . .

Yes, there's still a Tolchester! It's different than in the days of the Gay Nineties, but you can rest assured that when Dave Bramble gets done with his plans . . . it will still be a great asset to the people of Kent County and many, many folks from far and near.

Kent County News, August 13, 1973

The creation of Tolchester Park began almost by fluke nearly a century earlier. In 1876, a Philadelphia Quaker family named Taggart, owners of a steamboat freight and excursion line on the Delaware River between Philadelphia and Chester, and along the Chesapeake & Delaware Canal, decided to widen their scope of operations to include Chesapeake Bay. Captain Calvin Taggart and E. B. Taggart, father and son, oversaw this expansion, and an enthusiastic protégé named William Conlyn Eliason bore the brunt of the leg work.

The Taggarts' initiative was meant to coincide with the projected completion of a railroad link across the peninsula to Chestertown. In the aftermath of the Civil War, a climate of economic optimism had revived the rail industry. Track laying began in Delaware in 1867, and was proceeding, albeit somewhat fitfully, through Maryland toward an as-yet-to-be-built shipping terminus ten miles southwest of Chestertown in the area known as Tolchester. The Taggarts—and presumably Eliason— understood the viability of a steamboat connection between Baltimore and the Eastern Shore for the fast transportation of agricultural (and bay) products one way, and industrial goods the other. But since the Taggarts were ahead of the railroad, it was up to them to obtain a toehold in the general vicinity, construct a pier and warehouses, and begin a scheduled steamboat run. Financial backing came from an old family friend of the Taggarts, one John M. Ambruster, from Camden, New Jersey, himself the

owner of two steamboat companies operating on the Potomac
out of Washington, D.C.

For his part, Ambruster purchased a bay-fronting 1051-acre
tract of land called Tolchester Farm in mid-July, 1876.[1] The tract
had ancient origins: in 1659, Cecilius Calvert, Lord Proprietor of
Maryland, had granted it to William Toulson, who was required
to pay, "by fealty . . . at the City of St. Mary's at the two most
usual feasts in the year, viz., at the Feast of the Annunciation . . .
and at the Feast of St. Michael the Archangel . . . the rent of ten
shillings nine pence halfpenny sterling silver or gold."[2] The
property—later known as the Mitchell Estate, after its manor
house (also called, at one time, Gresham Hall)[3]—had been di-
vided and recombined over the two centuries. Conveniently, in
1876 the tract came up for sale due to a property litigation. Once
the deed had been transferred to Ambruster, a pier was quickly
built and the side paddle wheeler Sarah K. Taggart was put into
service between Tolchester and Baltimore.

That particular steamboat turned out to be a poor choice because it wasn't configured to carry bulk freight, but a more dire
snafu resulted when the railroad went bankrupt. Track-laying
was permanently halted northwest of Chestertown near Worton,
ten miles from the pier. The dilemma thus posed was what to
do with (1) the Sarah K. Taggart, (2) the new pier at Tolchester,
(3) the leased wharf space in Baltimore, and (4) the huge Tolchester Farm tract. Ambruster, the Taggarts, and Eliason struck
upon a novel solution—novel because of who they were: an aging
businessman, two Quakers, and a Methodist teetotaler. They decided to create a beachside resort and park.

Public places earmarked for amusement, also known as
"pleasure gardens," were just coming into vogue in the United
States. Bathing resorts such as Long Beach Island in New Jersey,
Narragansett, and Coney Island, all long established, were adding mule-driven carousels, primitive Ferris wheels and roller
coasters, slides, bowling alleys, shooting galleries, horror houses,
and beer pavilions—and succeeding wondrously. The greater the
variety of diversions, the more crowds they drew. On the heels

of the psychically depressing Civil War, the public craved distraction. The notion of getting away from a frazzling city (or boring countryside) for a few hours of revelry and relaxation had universal appeal. On Chesapeake Bay, other day resorts were in the planning stages—Bay Ridge at the entrance to the Severn, Tivoli at the mouth of the Potomac. The tree-shaded bluff at Tolchester, in combination with its unspoiled beach, seemed a natural destination. Furthermore, Messrs. Ambruster, Taggart, and Eliason rightly assumed that an excursion by steamboat (at the time, crossing the Bay from Baltimore to Tolchester took just over two hours) would only add to the fun.

But a larger steamboat was needed for the passenger run, and a park, initially of modest proportions, had to be created. Lack of money proved to be an ongoing problem, so the Taggarts and Ambruster worked out a public stock purchase for their newly created Tolchester Steamboat Company. Eliason was put in command of a suitable paddle wheeler named *Pilot Boy*. At the Baltimore end, he was also in charge of advertising, for which he showed an early flair. Ambruster, meanwhile, spent the summer with his family on the Tolchester bluff to direct the creation of the picnic grounds, bath houses, and concession stands. By 1878, the following season, *Pilot Boy* was shuttling some six hundred passengers per trip—its capacity load—to and from the new Tolchester pier.

Though profitable, the fledgling business required the kind of financial expansion that its cash proceeds could not pay for. The pier had to be extended to a ten-foot depth at low tide, and there was pressure to add more buildings, entertainments, and concessions. Another steamer, *Nelly White*, with twice the tonnage of *Pilot Boy*, appeared on the scene. By 1882, in the course of underwriting the emendations, Ambruster had no choice but to mortgage, then sell off all but thirty acres of Tolchester Farm. When he died in 1884, his widow's share in stock and the deed to the thirty acres was bought back by the now heavily indebted company. In 1887, William C. Eliason, who had been general manager *de facto* since the firm's creation, engineered the formation of the new Tolchester Beach Improvement Company. The purchase price was $177,000, inclusive of

> the Hotel, Restaurant, Bath Houses, Stables, sheds, pavilions, bridges, wharves . . . all the furniture, beds and bedding, linens, tableware, kitchen utensils and Household articles of every description, tables, dishes, cutlery, stoves, and ranges which were in the hotel, and Restaurant on said 15th day of October 1887, also 500 bathing suits, the ice stored in the ice houses, all the flowers, plants, and chattels in the Hot House now on said tract of land. Also one Carousel complete, one set of Flying Horses, a Lot of Swings, 15 row boats, all the tables, benches, wagons, carts and implements.[4]

Tolchester Park's fame was spreading, thanks to Eliason's energetic promotions. A sample of his ad writing, from the *Baltimore Sun*, May 17, 1881, proclaimed that

> on or after May 25 . . . , the elegant excursion steamer Nellie [sic] White leaves from her new wharf, Pier 13, daily except Sunday. . . . Great improvements have been made at the beach and grounds. . . . NO LIQUORS ON BOATS OR GROUNDS. Excursion tickets 50 cents. Great inducements now offered to Sunday schools and societies. Apply to William C. Eliason, Agent, 112 Light Street Wharf.

Eliason's copy led to the most effective advertising of all: word of mouth. Ticket sales soared, and the park flourished as an entertaining and inexpensive family-oriented destination. But Eliason's chief contribution was his hands-on leadership as a steamboat company executive. Believing that the park's success hinged on a satisfying cruise in both directions, he saw to it, as the years passed and the century turned, that the pleasures of the excursion continued.

Writing in the *Baltimore Sun Magazine* in August 1978, Harry L. Tyson, a former Baltimore Gas & Electric employee, reminisced about a company picnic in May 1923. The boat was the *Louise*, popularly known as "Belle of the Bay," one of the best-loved of all the Tolchester side paddle wheelers, then almost sixty years old (her iron keel had been laid in Wilmington, Delaware, in 1864), with a capacity of 2,500 people.

> When we reached Fort McHenry the band played "The Star Spangled Banner," and we all stood facing the fort.
> I carried my girl's wicker lunch basket and her coat. We found a spot on the upper deck, settling back in our chairs to enjoy the smell of salt-like air, coffee roasting, and even the smell of the coke ovens of the Bethlehem Steel Company.
> The excursion was all so new and wonderful for us as we walked around the three decks of the boat and talked with friends. Some of the men from the Electric Distribution Department played cards. Others watched other ships pass on their way in and out of the harbor. Captain Kolb brought the *Louise* in, barely touching the Tolchester pier. After the gangplank was down the passengers walked down the pier and up a hill to a shady place where picnic tables were available.

Tyson's day at Tolchester began with the consumption of the contents of the wicker basket—variety and portions all fondly remembered because "nobody counted calories." Following lunch, he and his friends watched a ball game featuring cross-dressing on the part of fellow workers of both sexes.

> . . . the girls [wore] dark bloomers and middy blouses with wide black ties, and the boys dressed as girls (flappers).

Then came a tug-of-war between the Electric Department and the Gas Department. Tyson doesn't specify which team won. Meanwhile, children of employees held potato sack and wheelbarrow races; in the latter instance, "one child held the feet of another who raced on his hands."

> A clown gave the children candy and Farson's Band lined up parade style and led a long line around the park.

We also enjoyed a ride on the carousel and tried to get the brass ring for a prize. Then it was the Ferris wheel, the racer dip, and several trips through the Tunnel of Love.

The afternoon of fun was brought to a conclusion with a swim in Chesapeake Bay. Tyson especially remembers the two-piece rented suits—which "today would be at a museum"—because the *Sunpaper* he had bought for two cents that very morning reported how one-piece bathing suits had just been permitted in Atlantic City. Tolchester's fashion lag notwithstanding, the swim was a refreshing experience. All too soon it was time to head back to the wharf for the return trip to Baltimore.

Just about sunset, after we found a place on the upper deck, near the pilot house, Captain Kolb pulled the whistle cord and we sailed home into the sunset.

There was dancing in the beautiful ballroom of the *Louise*, but up on the dark upper deck there was some singing and lots of snuggling.

Forty-two years later, in my imaginary walk with Messrs. Ward and Deringer through the abandoned park in 1965, I'm conjuring up snatches of the old excitement. In the gusty March emptiness, I find myself hanging on to every one of Mr. Ward's words as he brings the long-ago summers back to life. He is telling, for instance, about a fellow named William McCleary, who, though deaf and dumb and blind,[5] gave goat-cart rides around a small track until 1936. The ride cost a nickel. Mr. Ward relates that McCleary repaired all his harnesses, could put up and plumb a fence, and "rake leaves, same as you and me." This leads Mr. Ward to reminisce about the sundry horse and pony rides that were phased out because of too many broken arms and legs.

A fellow named Gus Warner managed a fish tank, where the hooking of a satisfactory number of wooden fish resulted in a prize. In 1925, a man known as T. L. Stein introduced small-scale automobiles, called Custer Cars, that ran on a loop of track. Ned Nolan, who built and operated the bowling alley dating from the turn of the century, was also responsible for creating the ever-popular railroad in 1880. Pointing to the old dance hall, later to become a roller-skating rink, Mr. Ward recounts how an orchestra from one of the steamboats performed there from 1 until 3 P.M. (the busy musicians also performed on the journey from Baltimore, at the hotel for lunch, at the pavilion after the dance hall, and finally on the boat going home). Nearby, the café that had opened around 1900 was still in operation on closing day in 1962. Excursionists could sample various other amusements, such as tall swings, a miniature golf course, a lakelet that held a fleet of stubby gasoline-engined boats, an Ocean Dip slide, and a bath-house complex (through which seven hundred people passed in a single day), in addition to the ever-popular bathing beach and picnic groves.

And there was more. Around 1880, a harness-racing track opened—a venue met with instant success, although the temperance-minded management frowned upon the betting that accompanied the racing. The track closed in 1914 and was converted to a baseball field. Later, the facility was used for the first electrically illuminated night games between the softball leagues of Kent and Queen Anne's Counties. An exhibition hall sometimes referred to as The Annex displayed homemade products, including jams and jellies, canned preserves, farm produce, and hand-sewn crafts. A fake Indian teepee village perched on the banks of a ravine behind the bluff. There was a tot's boat merry-go-round in a circular pond, a Victorian bandstand,[6] the Ferris wheel,[7] and a bustling Lower Dairy Bar located just off the wharf, where eager arrivers and weary departers could get a quick pick-me-upper. The Tolchester Fair was held every August, often breaking attendance records (in 1899, for example, the three-day event attracted 28,300 people). Highlights included a livestock show, Ladies Day (when women's handiwork was on display and judged), a horse show, a jousting tournament, a championship baseball game, and a cooking exhibit featuring a huge cake along with its recipe, which listed a chapter and verse of the Bible referring to each of its ingredients.

Materially, the park's attractions were added to until about 1935. Before then, despite the onset of the Great Depression, the enthusiasm of the crowds continued to warrant the expenditure. The park boasted something for everyone; at the height of the season, five boats from Baltimore steamed daily to Tolchester's wharf. The steamboats regularly carried passengers above their rated capacities—up to three thousand on a single crossing. But in 1936, the Tolchester Beach Improvement Company, which still owned and operated the park and the steamers (and also owned several wharves off Light Street in Baltimore's Inner Harbor), went into receivership. While attendance receipts were holding steady, the business climate had become dubious. The boats had developed a host of problems due to old age, and the park itself was sorely in need of capital outlays.

Then, as the United States became embroiled in World War II and the boats were made available for troop conveyence, scheduled passenger service from Baltimore was suspended. Although many Eastern Shore residents were still arriving by car, now on rationed gas, attendance at the park took a significant dip. Despite misgivings on the part of the management, beer was introduced in the café in 1941; it was a hit, but the decision prompted the company's teetotaling director, the son of William C. Eliason, to resign. No longer the focus of family excursions and Sunday School picnics, the amusement park began to attract a rougher crowd. After the War, a much-curtailed steamer schedule further reduced the sagging attendance. Ownership changes and financial mismanagement followed, until the park became a liability to its creditors. At one point, to satisfy an overdue loan, the merry-go-round with its calliope and carved animals was disassembled and carted away. (Later, the animals were sold to collectors and museums for many times more than the amount of the original debt.) As the superannuated amusements folded one by one, maintenance of the physical plant was neglected. Paint chalked and peeled on walls and balustrades, the wharf became splintery, the train began to rust. The slow but inexorable decline of the once-thriving park accelerated with the opening of the Bay Bridge in 1952. The park's final few years of life were indeed a shabby affair. In the spring of 1962, the sole remaining steamer, *Bay Belle*, now operating only sporadically between Baltimore and Tolchester, went on cold iron. Five months later, the owners announced that the park would not reopen the following summer.

Looking at the photographs taken in 1965, I can readily understand, as Mr. Ward intimates, how the park will never die in the minds of people who went there. By now, I practically count myself among their number. I've pored over plenty of other, earlier photographs, too.

Among my favorites is one dating from the late 1940s, taken from the upper deck of a docked steamer, toward which a throng of excursionists is streaming to board. Women are wearing summer frocks and two-piece suits. Men—with the exception of one or two appearing uncomfortably warm in business attire—are in shirtsleeves. Some people are looking down at their feet, so as not to stumble on the uneven planks of the pier. But whether they're looking down or up, or inwardly, or just plain gazing out into space, almost everyone is smiling. They've had a great day and done all the things they set out to do, and now they're readying for the return trip across the bay.

The happiest-looking person is a trim-figured, well-coiffed woman with a suitcase in one hand and the hand of a little girl in the other. To me, this woman is a metaphor for something I can't quite put my finger on—motherhood? sex goddess? feminine ideal? She and her daughter must have spent the night in one of the hotel's thirty-four bedchambers, and quite possibly—once the child was asleep—a lover tiptoed into the room. He could have been the sailor in dress whites, his neckerchief a black wishbone, who's grinning jauntily a few steps behind. Two teenage girls are gesticulating so animatedly that their hands blur. Along the foreshortened wharf, people diminish in size until they become a mosaic of hats and faces. Everybody in the foreground is carrying something: a man his suit jacket, another man a jug cooler, a woman her baby, a woman a picnic hamper, a woman her sweater, the sailor an overnight bag. Another woman is toting a bulging sack perhaps containing stuffed animals won as prizes.

Innocently unaware of the camera, this bevy of excursionists is a cross-section of Baltimore's white middle class—content, well fed, not averse to returning to the daily grind. They've taken their fill of recreation, and as they sail back across the bay, they'll reflect on what a pleasant visit it has been. When they return to Tolchester—for return they will, the way they're feeling now—they'll revel in the old thrills and leisures as connoisseurs. Meanwhile, at bay level in a visually disconnected aside similar to that of a Brueghel painting, a party of three in a rowboat navigates next to a piling.

That a park like Tolchester's would evolve and thrive for nearly seven decades, then die a death of attrition over the span of two more before disappearing from the face of the earth, seems almost fabulous to a latecomer like me. Although I've turned away from the photographs and am back in the present— too firmly so, it seems—I actually miss the old park. I never witnessed it except vicariously, never rode its rides or partook of its concessions, but I miss the idea of it. Even though I take some consolation from the presence of the well-appointed marina and housing development that stand phoenix-like in the park's stead, I grieve for the loss of Americana. If only one structure—the pavilion, for example—had been left as evidence of Tolchester's extraordinary past, the present might not seem so . . . ordinary. But such is the glamour of a thing gone—that which remains can't hold a candle to it.

The Tolchester I never saw delivered a quantum of pleasure utterly foreign to the present. In season after summer season it positively sizzled with excitement. People arrived by the tens of thousands, eager for a good time. Plenty of hard luck may have been cursed at the shooting range and the bowling alley, and plenty of hearts may have been broken after false promises in the

Tunnel of Love, but overall, Tolchester stood for the collective deliverance of grace. It served as an antidote to the humdrum induced by the Industrial Age, which delivered nothing but societal security redeemable by endless hard work. For travail-surfeited Baltimoreans, the voyage across the Bay substituted bliss for drudgery. The getaway that was Tolchester was also a gateway—an entrance to a land removed from everything that dragged down the human spirit.

Today, there's nothing left of any of it, and memory itself has been diluted, if not distorted, by the passage of time. As the American way of life plodded onward into the future, the old amusements were replaced by newer ones: fast cars and modern household appliances and split-level homes in newly created suburbs. To continue the candle analogy, Tolchester burned for a long time—right down to the candlestick, in fact—and then it was snuffed out. Other destinations grabbed Baltimoreans' attention, most notably Ocean City and its satellite beaches on the Atlantic shore. The road trip itself became a form of entertainment, with motels, restaurants, drive-in movies, and scenic wonders all suddenly accessible. Speeding along the highway at sixty miles per hour made the eight knots or so of a walking-beam side paddle wheeler seem barely moving. Then, too, the pleasure-boating boom after World War II turned upper Chesapeake Bay into a vast aquatic playground, whereas formerly it had served as a cruising area only for the yacht-owning rich.

But the biggest change, I think, was the advent of television, which gave people the option of amusing themselves right in their own living rooms. The midway just couldn't compete with the channel selector. Thanks to their exposure to television, Americans began to think globally, whether they wanted to or not, and ironically, television also spurred them to vacation farther from home. Bigger and better pleasure gardens were waiting to be experienced: places like Disneyland, Six Flags, Busch Gardens, where state-of-the-art complexly engineered thrills made the old fare seem tame. Contemporary theme parks still strive to outdo each other in their zeal to convey paying customers almost out of their heads—almost, but not quite. This seems to be the criterion nowadays for coming back for more.

Strolling alone late at night along the lightless avenues, between parked cars and service entrance poles, beneath a canopy more aptly characterized as outer space than sky, I fall prey to feelings of nostalgia. The last echoes of the old hubbub have long since died away. Between dark bungalow corners buttressed by even darker shrubbery, only pale television flickerings bounce off the window panes. Out in the shipping channel and beyond, spreads a silvery silence, informationally delineated by the red and green winking of buoys. Greater Baltimore is an inverted bowl of orangy pink with faint pinpricks of light along the distant shoreline. Quiet though my footsteps be, canine misinterpretation makes them suspect; nobody is supposed to be out of doors at this hour. The barking begins, first one wakeful watchdog, then another. I could be a thief stealing the night itself, so out of place am I. Motion-detecting floodlights suddenly glare. Electronically, I'm being subjected to surveillance and warned off—but I haven't done anything wrong! Mosquitoes police the proximity of my bare flesh. A homeowner lets in his dog—one less basso in the incriminating chorus. Along these umbrageous communal blocks where absolutely nothing is going on save family business behind closed doors, my aloneness seems to conspire against me. The longer I walk, the more I pay the price of nonconformity. The message I'm receiving loud and clear is that it's time to head back home and go to bed.

On one such midnight ramble, I go to Ohio Beach and strike up a conversation with a lone surf fisherman who's pulling in one large catfish after another, as fast as he cares to bait the hook. He's at the waterline of the concrete boat ramp—an archetypal figure pursuing a timeless avocation. By his clothes and car, I see he's a poor man. His wife is sitting in the car, evading the night chill, and there may be a child asleep in the back seat.

The man appears glad for my company; he tells me the cats have never run better. He's sharing the good news in case I want to go back for my own tackle and bait.

His luck is due, he guesses, to a beneficial conjunction of moon and tide, and to underscore his point, he opens the lid of the cooler beside him and shows me his catch thus far: at least a dozen two-foot-long bull-headed creatures, bewhiskered and glistening, stacked like cordwood. By his estimate, he has fifty pounds of the bay's finest, freshest protein. As we get to talking, I confess that even though I'm not much of a fisherman, at some unspecified time in the future—maybe if hard times hit—I might become one. He laughs, says he can't remember when hard times *haven't* hit him. I tell him how my wife recently bought some catfish fillets at the supermarket and that, despite her culinary efforts, they didn't taste very good.

"Yah, it got to be fresh, or it ain't worth fixin'," he concurs. There ensues a discussion of cat's delicate flavor, which we both hold in high esteem, and some favorite methods of preparation.

Because his cooler is so full and the hour is so late, he's not overly assiduous; he casts easily, and as soon as his sinker plops into the water, like as not he'll wedge the butt of his pole between the blocks of concrete. When a nibble shakes the pole, he tends to ignore it, which means that he is often re-baiting the line—not that he minds in the least—but every once in a while the unattended pole does a full-fledged Saint Vitus' dance, at which point he casually grabs it, locks the reel, and gives the pole a hard over-the-shoulder backward jerk, firmly hooking the nibbler, and then there follows a textbook reeling-in until another round-eyed, slack-jawed victim dangles helplessly, ready for the pliers. He shows me how to hold the broad fish so as not to get fingers sliced open by its sharp lateral fins, and invites me to try, but I point out, rightly so, that his own hands are twice the size of mine. In one smooth motion, he removes the hook from the cartilage of the fish's mouth and, kicking open the lid of the cooler, drops the hapless creature inside. The catfish hardly flops—I don't think it quite realizes it has been caught. Two or three more of its size, and the lid won't shut. This is turning out to be the luckiest of nights.

He tells me how he once caught a twenty-two-pounder, using ten-pound test, off the bridge at Chestertown. Ever so gingerly, he had to walk the snagged, still-swimming fish to the far end of the bridge, whereupon he handed the pole to his wife and he himself went down below to the riverbank with a dip-net. The weight of the fish bent the rim of the net. It must have been the granddaddy of Chester River cats; its hide was gray with moss, but he swore it was as succulent and sweet-tasting as any of its grandchildren.

When I inquire about what will become of tonight's gargantuan catch, he says that when he and his wife get home, they'll fillet every fish, then stow most of them in the freezer. "But tomorrow, oh man, a fish-fry for sure!" I'm happy to hear his plans—happy for him and happy for myself. Gabbing with a stranger on such a fine evening has made me forget the loss of Tolchester Park and its long-silent steam whistles and shrieks of delight. The fisherman is enjoying himself, and so am I. His stories, his expertise, and our chance camaraderie have been superlatively entertaining, and so has the night—the breeze off the bay and the licking wavelets, our joshing good-byes, my walk back home, the sound of my footfall on familiar gravel, the moon, the slight shiver of adrenaline when a rabbit or raccoon rustles in the roadside bushes. I ask myself rhetorically: what *don't* I do for amusement?

chapter
10

It's a bit simplistic to say that the bayside provides the place or space for "getting away from it all," because if anything, it offers just the opposite. Here, almost too much is going on to get away from. Why tune it out anyway, when it's all so fascinating?

On the crisscrossing thoroughfares above and beyond the bluff, the processions and processionals are never-ending. Add to these the companionate sound of the incoming wind temporarily notched between zephyr- and gale-force, the thudding of waves, gull cries, goose honks, eagle and osprey whistles, insect riffs, the intensifying and diminishing engine racket on the water and in the air—and it's no idyll for the effects-weary, no place to run to and hide. Tritely put, there's never a dull moment. Yet, this *is* a quiet place, quiet because it affords peace within me. It's paradoxical to say that my even keel is dependent upon so rich a diet of stimulation and tranquillity, but it happens to be true. Witnessing the busy spectacle encourages me to think, and when I'm able to do that, I feel secure.

This west-facing bluff is a refuge to me. I've grown comfortable with my self-appointed duties as Nature-observer, marine aficionado, and weather maven rolled into one. The quicksilver surround, absorbing in its totality, is mind-occupying in its least part as well. I could study the baby toads in the garden or the pebbles on the beach all day if I wanted to. In such an intensely evocative setting, there's nothing too minor to be dismissed as uninteresting. Even though part of me may forever remain an inland innocent—charmed by Chesapeake ambience, awed by coastal splendor—I've also lived here long enough to take it all in stride.

I wish my father could see it here; he was the one who implanted the idea of a refuge in me at a tender age. He was always talking about his own refuge, a place away from the demands of his career as a college professor. I think he finally found it, in retirement, under a live oak tree in his backyard garden in Florida. I suppose I grew up believing that, at some point, I would stumble upon my own refuge, and now that I have, I'm assuming it would meet with his approval. At the very least, he'd appreciate its remove from the automotive snarl and corporate-logo'd sprawl. As for Nature, he'd imbibe that, too, and in as large draughts as possible. But this is a place he'll never see, except in those family-circulated packets of snapshots we bring with us when we visit him, because he doesn't get out anymore, and seeing as he sees now, it doesn't matter much what he looks at. In his eighty-seventh year, my father is in his terminal refuge: an Alzheimer's unit in a nursing home in North Carolina, some ten hours away by car. Checking on him as infrequently as I do heaps filial guilt upon my head and shoulders, as if I were upending a bucket of the stuff each time I allow myself a thought of the shrunken, withered shell of a formerly robust man. But what's to be done? Caring for him in our home at this stage of his debilitation is out of the question. He needs skilled twenty-four-hour tending, plus a regular dose of a mood enhancer, lest in his confused anxiety, he wander off and really get himself into trouble. My father no longer knows my name (nor his own), and it's a toss-up whether he would recognize who I am (or any other family member), but there he is, day after day, month after month, victim of his own longevity, grown fond of bland dining-hall turkey soup and custard, medicated to a permanent plateau of serenity.

His refuge, if he still has one, is something that nobody can assess, much less analyze, anymore; mine materializes from what's in front of me, and is accessible to anybody who's been here. My shelter from danger and distress, in offering balm to my psyche, so stimulates my senses that I have to ask myself from time to time, what exactly am I being sheltered from? It isn't the wind that whips the wave tops white, making me feel as though I'm being pushed through life, blown along like a fallen leaf. It isn't the sun, so sharp at midday from the water's reflection that I have to confine my movements to oases of shade. It isn't the bay view that, while mesmerizing, rubs in the fact that environmental pollution is daily tightening the screws on the fate of humanity. No, it is the sum of these and everything else—the oddly calming effect that comes from witnessing more than enough.

Others have also singled out Tolchester as their refuge of choice, and I can understand why. It's easy to settle into a place where the past is all but forgotton; the future seems immaterial, as if it'll never arrive. Except for the manifold sensory inputs of which I speak, nothing much happens around here. The status quo is upheld year after year after year. The community is too young to be gentrified, too old to be modernized, too heterogeneous to be type-cast, and too far off the beaten path to be targeted as a growth area. As ever, the refuge is in knowing that Chesapeake Bay is its prime constant, an unchanging everchanging presence that is pleasurable to live beside, and inland from the water is farmland on a vast and lonesome scale. Tolchester is that rare thing: a waterfront community left to its own devices.

Picture the residents' collective shock, then, when a private corporation composed of former top officials in Maryland's environmental administration announces a plan to create a dredging spoils disposal area on two adjacent farms. The proposed site, totaling in excess of five hundred and fifty acres, is a portion of the very land William Toulson was deeded in 1659—acreage that was surveyed and gridded for an expanded Tolchester Estates back in the 1920s but has thus far remained planted in corn.

The man who purchased both tracts from the Mendinhall heirs still farms them today, but he's in his seventies and wants to quit. Like most farmers, he is known to gripe about how it's next to impossible to make a living anymore. This summer's drought has only added to his woes; if it continues, he stands to lose his shirt, as he tells anyone who'll listen. Such poormouthing clashes, of course, with every perceived indicator of his prosperity: the fine house, the new pickup truck for him and luxury sedan for his wife, the latest and largest in field equipment, the aggressive applications of herbicides and pesticides . . . his list of spending goes on and on. Yet as he tells it, any day now, his whole operation will go belly-up.

Like a typical farmer, too, he's anticipating a tidy profit from the liquidation of his real estate holdings once he gives up farming. The traditional route to making a profit off farmland has been to subdivide, usually with the assistance of a developer, beginning with roadside lots and gradually working toward the back forty—all the while turning a deaf ear to cries of "sellout" by density-phobic neighbors. But this field-weary agrarian has chosen a more socially sensitive route: the first thing he has done is to obtain a conservation easement for one of the two farms. In exchange for $198,000, paid to him by a nonprofit land preservation agency, he has permitted a clause to be inserted in the property deed stipulating that the land must be used for agricultural purposes only. This devalues the farm somewhat because it limits a potential buyer's options; no short-term investor or land speculator, for example, will go near it. Yet the farmer gains long-term credibility in the eyes of those who fear runaway residential growth in Kent County, the self-styled "Jewel of the Chesapeake." By retaining its agricultural stamp, the farm is spared the fate of becoming a Levittown.

In a strange twist, this is precisely what the farmer intends to do with his other tract: carve it up into as many building lots as the zoning plan allows. The land's residential zoning status is already on the books (and has been since the 1920s), so there's nothing to petition for, nothing to warrant a public hearing. The farmer is satisfied as far as his conscience is concerned; the one property will remain as it is—providing him with an early cash windfall from the preservationists, no matter what it sells for later—and the other property will guarantee an even better dividend that'll ensure him and his wife a cushy retirement.

But then comes along the sweeter deal. The corporation that's bidding on the disposition of dredging spoils has been looking for just such a site. The lure is enticing: sell the two farms to the corporation, the former Maryland state officials urge him, and he'll be paid *ten times* the going rate for farm acreage.

The farmer must feel very foolish as he explains how he's already put a conservation easement on the one property, while the other is zoned residential. No problem, the entrepreneurs quickly assure him. *Both* farms will retain their agricultural status. This is what is known as a creative environmental solution! The farmer scratches his head, perplexed. He doesn't quite understand how—in the jargon of bay dredging—an upland disposal site can be used for agriculture. It's easy, the former officials tell him, it just takes a little reconfiguring of the topography. Here's what will be done: the topsoil will be scraped into a fifteen-foot berm around the perimeter of the combined acreage; then, in the course of six or seven winter dredging seasons, spoils slurry will be pumped through a pipeline from offshore barges into the resultant basin—about 2.5 million cubic yards, amounting to a couple of feet spread over the entire expanse each year—to be gradually dewatered (via a gravity pipeline back to the bay) and dried so as to form a series of successive crusts. And here's some more good news: certain grasses and cover crops can be grown on reclaimed silt. Possibly, even rice paddies could be established as well. When the accumulated spoils reach the top of the berm, the resultant elevated field, if re-veneered with topsoil, should support almost any crop. So, the farms will stay in agriculture all the while and be returned to full productive capacity in the end. Pretty nifty plan, huh? Or, better yet, a permanent park could be superimposed—woods, thickets, wildflower meadows, wending paths with benches—with an excellent view of the bay.

The project proposers frankly admit that an upland disposal project of this magnitude has never been attempted before. This is going to be a first! The farmer and his wife think it over awhile. They've been in the community a long time, and even though they can almost taste that suddenly-within-their-grasp refuge in the Caymans, they want to do right by their neighbors. Slowly increasing the altitude of five hundred and fifty acres with channel-bottom ooze sounds downright dicey. On the rural plain, the resultant monolith will stick out like an errant mesa, and Tolchester will be in its shadow. What about the groundwater beneath it, the farmer asks? Won't the salinity of the spoils runoff seep right through to the aquifer and pollute the wells? What about storm drainage? What if the berms are breeched after heavy rain?

Whoa! Too many questions all at once! *We're not here to answer every "what if," Mr. Farmer; we're here to offer you a pile of money.* The former officials concede that they haven't amassed all the hard data, but they swear they'll undertake the project with the utmost responsibility and sensitivity from start to finish. What they need to do right away is dig core samples in the target subsoil. If there's a clay substrate, the risk of downward seepage is nil—simple as that. So, with the farmer's permission, a backhoe is hired for an afternoon; in eighteen test holes, a clay layer (its thickness and extensiveness unspecified) is proven to exist. With we-told-you-so glee, the former officials proclaim the presence of a natural clay liner—clay that, if need be, can be extended up the inside of the berm. Additionally, bentonite can be trucked in, or plastic sheeting can be substituted—whatever.

The glib talk, the several million dollars proffered, and the abjuration of creating a liability for the neighborhood work their magic. The farmer and his wife sign an option to sell both farms. They have no idea of the firestorm of negative publicity they're about to unleash, or the pariahs they're about to become—she thinks that she'll never have to hear him grumble about crop losses again, and he thinks that he'll never have to hear her complain about his long hours in the fields.

The dumping plan's next goal is the tentative approval of the Kent County commissioners, so that the necessary federal and state environmental permits can be applied for. By now, the news services have picked up the story; a spate of articles in *The Baltimore Sun* incites general alarm and outcry. Not only are the former officials chastised for insider impropriety, but their choice of an upland site is called into question. In the Chesapeake region, dredging spoils in the tens of millions of cubic yards have customarily been relegated to deepwater disposal. South of the Bay Bridge, for instance, an area known as Deep Trough served the purpose well until environmentalists began to raise objections about pollutants on the bay floor. Meanwhile, a startling tidbit of financial information is leaked: the former state officials stand to make *one hundred million dollars* from contracts with the State of Maryland and the Army Corps of Engineers.

In the initial public hearing, the former officials portray their plan as an economic development project. Let the Jewel of the Chesapeake accept the spoils, they say, and it will reap several million dollars up front, plus hundreds of thousands more in permit fees and annual taxes. At this point, two of the three county commissioners give the impression that they favor the proposal. An editorial in the weekly *Kent County News* shrilly concurs that, hard-strapped as the county is, the deal is too good to turn down. In disgust, a number of local individuals pen letters of rebuttal. This is mine:

To the Editor:
The proposal to pump dredging spoils on the two farms situated beside the community of Tolchester is truly symptomatic of the demonic callousness that big money can engender. [Your] craven editorial . . . attempts to focus the issue for all the wrong reasons. At issue is not an uphill battle for permits and approvals leading to the wishful enrichment of the Kent County coffers. At issue is the deliberate destruction of a modest bayside community.

For this is what will surely happen to Tolchester if such a proposal is facilitated, then implemented. A geographically isolating system of huge berms containing an elevated wasteland, the stinking odor of 500-plus acres of freezing/thawing, slowly drying muck, the unbearable noise of 'round-the-clock pumping, the salinization of the groundwater, the proliferation of obnoxious scavengers, the decimation of property values (and tax base), and the general unsavoriness of living next door to a spoils management facility of unprecedented size—all these will conspire to doom this place I call home.

Moreover, the local habitat of the bald eagle and other endangered species will be disrupted, if not destroyed.

But it is the human habitat I mostly worry about. That a politically tainted outfit . . . can, in effect, dispose of a community like Tolchester should put all Kent Countians on notice. We have a moral duty to prevent this environmentally irresponsible idea from getting beyond the planning stages, for if it ever becomes a reality, Tolchester itself will turn into a tragedy, a 21st-century Love Canal. . . .

Faced with an onslaught of negative opinion and commentary, the former Maryland state officials don't appear to be fazed in the least. They've come to the private sector with a mandate to make megabucks; they know the ins and outs of steering a project like this through at the highest levels. With extensive contacts in Annapolis, they've capitalized on the fact that the governor has given top-priority urgency to finding a place to dump dredging spoils. The process of widening and deepening the shipping channels never stops—Baltimore's viability as a port in the twenty-first century depends on it. The Tolchester Channel alone needs to be emptied of millions of cubic yards of silt, and the S-curve south of buoys #28 and #29 is scheduled for a massive recontouring. Across the bay, the disposal site at Hart-Miller Island is more than full; dewatered spoils there are layered to twice the height originally planned. Although there's talk of creating artificial islands in the upper bay, the idea is unpopular with boaters who like the wide-openness of the water. Evershrinking, almost-disappeared Poplar Island, south of Kent Point, is another possibility, but the transportation costs are prohibitive on a large scale.

On paper, the upland Tolchester site makes sense because it's right beside the channel to be dredged. If the people in the neighborhood can be convinced that their quality of life will not be adversely affected, the entrepreneurs figure they'll be home free.

To this end, a folksy, fact-minimizing public relations campaign is begun, with the former officials setting up a series of one-on-one meetings. Casually dressed (with the chauffeur-driven Cadillac parked around the corner), they knock on doors, soft-pedaling the juggernaut-to-be. But the Tolchesterites aren't fooled. The community has swallowed so many unfulfilled promises over the years—most recently, the malodorous sewage pumping facility that was deemed to be too high-tech to emit anything as low-tech as the smell of shit—that any new proposal, no matter how beneficial it purports to be, is met with reflexive skepticism.

Around this time, several property owners who live down private lanes that run between the two farms incorporate a protest committee. These people have the most to lose: their homes will be literally surrounded, if not suffocated, by the fifteen-foot-tall containment dikes. More steamroller than bandwagon, the committee is vociferous and well organized. The fight will be taken to the highest regulatory levels, then through the courts, if necessary. Each charter member contributes five thousand dollars to a war chest to pay for legal fees. An acronym is devised, memberships are solicited, petitions signed, neon-colored flyers circulated. A Washington advertising firm is hired to design a poster that depicts a row of ripe golden corn about to be buried under an avalanche of gray glop. The clarion call for citizen opposition echoes throughout Kent County, causing all three county commissioners to register immediate and unqualified disapproval of the dredge spoils plan.

Sensing that a change of strategy is needed, the former state officials announce their willingness to present their proposal to the Tolchester Community Association. On the specified Saturday afternoon, the turnout is astounding. I hadn't realized so many people resided here—or so many cars. Due to the relative dearth of folding chairs in the community hall, a full third of the audience either stands or sits on the floor. I notice several reporters in attendance, as well as the local delegate to the state legislature. Surely, a crowd of this size is a first for the Community Association, which rarely gathers together a quorum (twenty members would do) at its infrequent palavers.

Behind a folding table laden with slick informational hand-outs sits one of the former officials and his lawyer. The two men look pleasant and noncommittal, like regular middle-aged guys you'd think of as neighbors, not as rapacious outsiders eager to clinch a multi-million-dollar deal that'll spell disaster for the community. After being introduced by the chairperson, the former official outlines the disposal plan in an upbeat manner, sunnily enunciating his words. He stresses the negligible impact it will have on all concerned and the rigorous environmental standards to which it will adhere. He refers to the berms as "dunes," tastefully landscaped so as not to intrude on the surroundings. Within the dunes will lie a series of wetlands that'll attract many species of wildfowl, and when the wetlands dry out, they'll be tilled and planted in cover crops that'll grow lushly until harvested, and then the cycle of spoils pumping will repeat itself. At all seasons of the year, he avers, the site will be beautiful to behold.

He assures everyone that Maryland Environmental Service, the quasi-public agency that will be contracted to run the facility, has a proven record of integrity. Over time, as the level of land rises, new agricultural procedures will be experimented with and new crops will be sown. Who knows, Tolchester may become the home of wondrous advances in seed genetics, to benefit areas of the world where land reclamation is a life-or-death struggle. And in six to eight years, when the dunes are full, the resultant plateau can be converted into that nice park.

The former official goes on to say that he realizes how intimidating the term *dredging spoils* can be. He prefers to refer to it as *silted material*, for it is nothing but good topsoil washed into, and settled at the bottom of, the bay. A portion of what lies at the bottom of the Tolchester Channel comes from Kent County's own shores, and the rest of it washes down from Pennsylvania and New York. It's a pure, clean deposit—slightly saline, to be sure—ready to be put right back to use. Every bargeload pumped ashore will be monitored for contamination, and this is more than a promise: it's a federally mandated regulation. And not to worry, the site *will not* accept Baltimore harbor silt that contains heavy metals and other toxic pollutants.

And speaking of pumping, he adds, the decibel level of the offshore pumps will be no more intrusive than that of a muffled generator. The piping system will be mostly buried, so as not to mar the landscape. The dewatering pipes will end far out in the bay, and only crystal-clear runoff will flow from them. As for the layers of drying silt, there will be no odor other than a faint low-tide smell during the months of active pumping, December through March, when most folks keep their windows closed anyway.

The skeptics in the audience—my wife and I among them— are shaking their heads and rolling their eyes. Sensing antagonism to his sugar-spun fantasy, the former official deftly shifts gears, announcing that he and his lawyer have come primarily to listen. He sincerely believes the community has been presented with a good plan, a fair plan, a generous plan—which he'll be more than happy to discuss further with any concerned individual— but now he wants to hear what we, the residents of Tolchester, have to say. He entreats us to be open-minded. We are being offered an asset, not a liability. The advantages will more than offset any temporary inconvenience.

Immediately, a man jumps up: "What advantages? You're feeding us a bunch of hogwash! You're just a goddamn politician, forcing us to accept something nobody else wants. I know I'm speaking for everyone in this room—you've nothing to offer us but crap! Why don't you just go away?"

Another man: "Yeah, we don't want your dredge spoils—not now, not ever. You can pack up your bag, Santa Claus, and get the hell outta here!"

The hall erupts in applause. "Order! Order!" shrieks the chairperson. "This meeting cannot continue until order is restored!"

She has no gavel but her voice, which pierces the din only to the extent that she can call on the next person who's waiting to sound off. The former official and his lawyer exchange uncomfortable, vaguely concerned looks.

An elderly lady: "I've lived in Tolchester for forty-seven years, and I've seen some dumb proposals advanced—most defeated—but yours is the dumbest yet. I cannot for the life of me understand why anyone would want to situate a spoils dump right next to such a lovely community. Nobody stands to profit but you!"

Her neighbor to the left: "You politicians are all the same! You pretend to have solutions, but what you really have in mind is how best to fatten your own wallets. Go away, stay away, and don't ever come back!"

After the plaudit dies down, a further suggestion: "Why don't you take your plan across the bay to Aberdeen, where the U.S. government owns thousands of acres just sitting there unused? Or Pooles Island, closer to the channel still, where nobody goes anyway because it's full of of unexploded bombs? These are the sites you should be exploring."

A father with a squirmy two-year-old: "I live on Elm, one of the roads your so-called dune will be built along. What's going to keep my kid from climbing up and falling into the sludge and drowning? And who'll be held liable—you?"

Another dweller on Elm Road: "My home is all I got. It ain't much, but it's all mine. You have a lotta nerve, mister, to come in and talk about building this thing right next door. My property won't be worth jack, and you know it. You sure have a lotta nerve!"

His neighbor: "Do you have any idea how adversely this spoils dump is going to affect the value of *all* the real estate here? No prospective homeowner will go near Tolchester. None of us will be able to sell our homes—and for most of us, our homes represent our major investment, our sole equity."

Her follow-up: "Will your corporation be bonded to buy out the community, house by house and lot by lot, when your project turns into an ecological disaster?"

A young matron: "If I wanted to live beside a park—as you claim you could leave us with in eight years—I would have stayed in D.C. where parks are everywhere. I came here so my family and I could enjoy the bay and get away from the city. You've got nothing to offer us except a mountain of stinking gunk. You can call it any fancy name you want, but that's what it is."

"Park, schmark! You're bequeathing us an alternating dust-bowl and cesspool. And what'll we get in return—poisoned wells, air pollution, odor, noise, ugliness."

"Build it somewhere else! We don't want it here!"

"You intend to grow rich by making our lives miserable. That's a pretty low way of going about making money. Well, we've got news for you: we're going to stop this proposal of yours!"

"We'll fight it every step of the way! You better start thinking about putting the dump across the bay where you live, in your own backyard."

"What makes you think you can buy your way into Kent County, strewing false promises and destroying prime farmland all in the name of greed?"

"It reminds me of the old country tune: you get the gold mine, we get the shaft."

And so the scolding goes. When pressed, the former state official and his lawyer essay half-hearted explanations, but after a while, they deem it best to clam up. Questioned relentlessly, they begin replying: "We are not at liberty to divulge this information at this time." The former official gives the impression of being ill-prepared and out of his depth, his lawyer nothing but a yes-man. It's clear to everyone that a hundred-million-dollar scheme has been set in motion without addressing many of the crucial issues, nor has the extent of the opposition been gauged. Did these guys assume they were dealing with a bunch of naive hicks? Was the plan to come in here and do anything they wanted, expecting the residents to lie down and roll over?

Some two-and-a-half hours later, the dump-the-dump session terminates when the chairperson calls for a vote of acclaim. Are the attendees for or against the dredging spoils proposal? *All those in favor say aye*—the first silence of the afternoon de-

scends as if a mute button has been pressed. *All those against—*
once again, pandemonium reigns.

"The vote is unanimous. Meeting adjourned."

As the crowd surges toward the exit, the former official and
his lawyer stand up and get ready to leave. While their faces be-
tray some embarrassment, the glint in their eyes and the hunch
of their shoulders indicate that they're bracing for the long haul.
Like as not, they'll get their site, even if it means condemning
the two farms. In one scary unsettling moment, I realize that the
future of everybody's refuge hangs in the balance.

chapter

11

It is a foggy, airborne particle–enshrouded evening around midnight, and surrounding me are shadowy industrial colossi pinpricked with hundreds of electric lights. I'm standing beside the roaring updraft of Baltimore Gas & Electric's Wagner plant, fifteen miles across the bay from Tolchester. To my immediate left, beyond substations and a network of coal conveyors, are the soaring twin stacks of BGE's newer plant, Brandon Shores.

Nearly a mile in from the security gate, I've parked my car in the employees' lot and walked a couple of hundred feet to the water's edge. Although I've passed numerous caution signs, the last human being I saw was the security guard. Now I'm waiting at the bulkhead, a suitcase in hand. I'm about to ship out on the tugboat *Gulf Coast*, which hauls a coal barge continuously from Newport News to these energy-gobbling utilities that keep a major city twinkling in more ways than one.

A voyage on a tug is something I've always dreamed about, a quest that dates back to the time when I first learned to read. The adventure of the bathtub-plying *Little Tugboat*, which a young boy innocently set in a babbling brook and his dad later retrieved from the mouth of a big river, left a lasting impression on me. Now that I see tugboats every day from the bluff, I've become a bit of a rocking-chair expert. By their size and shape and towage, I can rattle off their names without resorting to binoculars.

But I've never been on one. And so, courtesy of Dann Marine Towing, Inc., a fifth-generation family-run business in Chesapeake City with a fleet of eleven tugs operating all along the eastern seaboard, I've arranged to board *Gulf Coast* and witness the tugging life firsthand.

As the brightly lit, tire-fendered tug with a yellow *D* on her stacks approaches, capturing me in her searchlights, I realize that there'll be no wharf from which to step aboard. Moments later, it dawns on me that there's no gangplank either. The BGE bulkhead has one rudimentary catwalk ending on a dolphin, or massed piling, from which I'll be required to leap—after heaving my overnight bag first—onto the tug's bow. All this I learn via gesticulations of the deckhands, who, as *Gulf Coast* nudges my precarious perch, offer their moral, if not physical support.

Gamely, I extend one leg across the void and push off with the other, landing not too off-balancedly on the tug's bulwarks, whereupon I jump down safely to the foredeck. Right off, I'm ushered into the deckhouse and shown my quarters—top bunk in a two-man woodgrain-paneled cabin with a dogged-down porthole. Next door is the head, and next to that is the galley, consisting of a large refrigerator and upright freezer, cabinets for drygoods and culinary items, a double stainless-steel sink (one side sudsy because crew members wash their own dishes), an electric stove with a custom-made corral around its top, a micro-wave oven, a toaster, and a prominent spice rack. The scarred countertop beside the stove doubles as a cutting board. Across from the galley is the table that seats the five-man crew. A small bronze plaque above the table announces that *Gulf Coast* was built in 1982 by Modern Marine Power, Inc., in Houma, Louisiana. On the opposite bulkhead is a recessed TV.

By way of orientation, I'm encouraged to eat whatever I choose whenever I want, go as I please, and keep whatever hours I feel comfortable with. I'm told that crew members stand watch six hours on and six hours off, twenty-four hours a day, seven days a week, and that everybody pitches in during docking and departure—but, as a visitor, I'm excluded.

Two decks up in the wheelhouse, I meet Jackie Nixon, relief captain on watch. He's bringing us alongside the BGE barge *E-4*, which is empty, or *light* in tug parlance, for the run south to

Newport News. Freshly painted black, *E-4* is a 3500-ton propulsionless oblong, lengthier than a football field and sixty-six feet wide, with a freeboard taller than two stories and an empty draft of about three feet. Her stern has an indentation, or *push notch*, and drooping off her slightly peaked prow is a wire cable bridle. She is one of five identical coal barges in BGE's fleet.

Jackie explains that once *Gulf Coast* is secured alongside, she'll draw *E-4* away from the pier and out into the channel. At this point, the tug will assume its towing position. The bridle is already attached to the towing cable, or *tow wire*, leading from the drum winch on the tug's afterdeck.

Everything seems to be happening quickly, although Jackie ambles casually between the forward and aft controls in the roomy wheelhouse. He has twenty-one windows for his viewing convenience, twenty-two if the window in the door is included. *Gulf Coast* isn't one of the mammoth tugs on the bay, but she's no shrimp boat either. Her hull is one hundred feet long, with a beam of thirty-two feet and a draft of thirteen feet, and in her engine room, a pair of Caterpillar D3512 diesels deliver 1200 horsepower apiece to each of her twin seventy-nine-inch screws. The dominant sensation aboard a tug, I soon learn, is one of engine proximity. Even in the wheelhouse, there's no escaping the clangor.

Jackie, fifty, a resident of Belhaven, North Carolina, is communicating by walkie-talkie with first mate Billy Cahoon, also from Belhaven, who is on the barge to direct the releasing of the lines. The tug stays alongside just long enough for Billy and a deckhand to climb down the ladder indentations in the barge's flank. It's well rehearsed, dangerous work, and it's over before I can fully grasp what happened. Jackie steers the tug around to the prow of the barge, thus drawing up the bridle on its short length—about a hundred feet—of tow wire, and we ease down the channel known as Brewerton Angle, past the shipyard and steelworks at Sparrows Point.

Soon we're in Brewerton Channel proper, passing North Point and heading for the cutoff to Craighill Channel Upper Range. Jackie turns over the helm to Billy and goes off watch. At twenty-three, Billy Cahoon is, by his own reckoning, one of the youngest first mates in bay tugging.

"The only bad thing about this wheelhouse job is that you can't get a suntan," he interjects while explaining the binnacle equipment. Contrary to the nomenclature, there is no ship's wheel, but rather a steering lever about six inches long, and even this is used only for close maneuvering. Most steering is done with the Sperry autopilot at the center of the console, between the magnetic compass and the port and starboard sets of engine controls. Course changing on autopilot means incrementally adjusting a small, flat knob. Miniaturization is evident elsewhere, too: on the overhead, the two monitoring radios—channel 13 (bridge to bridge) and channel 16 (calling and distress)—are each the size of Michener's *Chesapeake*, and the loud-hailer isn't much larger. Also mounted on the overhead are two small brass wheels for aiming the searchlights.

The complement of navigational accessories includes a Navionics DGPS chart navigator with a four-by-five-inch screen, capable of multi-mode settings that leave no question of course or position unanswered; two radarscopes left and right of the captain's chair (the one on the right, better for long distance, isn't functional at the moment); a Boatracs communicator for constant satellite tracking of *Gulf Coast*, which informs BGE and the coal terminal in Newport News of the tug's exact position and estimated time of arrival; a single side-band radio to the dispatcher's office in Chesapeake City; and a cellphone. About the only piece of equipment that's old-fashioned—and because it's old-fashioned, it's big—is a pair of 7 × 50 binoculars.

Once we're on Craighill Angle heading toward Craighill Channel, with all details secured, Billy walks over to the aft console and fires up the separate diesel engine of the tow winch. On the afterdeck, the deckhand on watch slips a flanged roller, called a *donut*, into place on the thickly greased Dutch, or chafing bar, that spans the breadth of the deck. On this will rest the inch-and-seven-eighths towing cable in extended position, so as not to abrade either itself or the aft bulwark. As soon as the deckhand releases the winch brake, Billy flips a lever to unwind the six-foot drum, lengthening the tow wire to around seven hundred feet. The prow of the empty barge slips far behind us, the middle section of the cable disappearing beneath our wake. The longer tow reduces stress on the fittings at both ends.

In this configuration, we will travel for some thirteen hours, at a speed of ten knots or so, depending on the current, at a steady 1740 engine revolutions per minute. The continuous barrage of diesel combustion gradually becomes less intrusive to my ears; when I listen carefully, I can even hear the plashing of the water. It's nearly two o'clock in the morning, and my immediate goal is to stay awake until we go beneath the Bay Bridge. I'm asking lots of questions, albeit tiredly, absorbing what information I can.

Our trip down the Chesapeake is marked by *waypoints*, places where the tug makes a course change. In a long nutshell, they are: Brewerton Angle, Craighill Angle, Craighill Channel, Craighill Entrance, Sandy Point, Bay Bridge, Thomas Point, buoy #83, buoy #78, Cove Point, Point No Point, Smith Point Light, buoy #62, Wolf Trap, York River Channel, Thimble Light (Thimble Shoal Channel), Old Point Comfort (Fort Wool), Newport News Channel, and the Pier Nine coal terminal. Billy's gently drawling phrases are succinct and factual. At each waypoint, an entry is made in the tug's log—the hour, latitude and longitude, magnetic compass heading, barometer, wind, sea, RPMs, speed in knots, and distance from the charted location.

My head is reeling from this late-night learning curve. We can see the center range lights on the Bay Bridge, directing us between the tallest pylons. A steady stream of eighteen-wheelers is crossing the bridge at this hour, oblivious to our lowly right-angled approach. Wearily, I slump on the wheelhouse stool—in contrast to Billy, who's bright and raring to converse, thanks to plenty of black coffee and cigarettes. At last, the twin spans with their curvaceous westward sweep pass overhead. I bid Billy goodnight and go below.

As per my request to be treated like one of the guys, it falls upon me to make up my own bunk. I'm shown the locker where sheets, blankets, and pillowcases are stored. There's a clothes washer and dryer on board, located in the fiddly, that excruciatingly loud passageway directly above the engine room. My bed linen is nothing to brag about (the blanket has burn holes and the sheets are frayed), but it's clean. In the lower bunk is David Evans, sound asleep. David's eighteenth birthday was yesterday. Arranging my bunk in semi-darkness, I do my best not to disturb him. Then I go next door to use the head and brush my teeth.

In shorts and T-shirt, I'm ready for the sack—but how do I climb to the top bunk? There's no ladder, no footholds anywhere. Bruising knee and shin, I cantilever myself from a storage locker onto the bunk rail, only to confront another problem: the air-conditioning vent is blowing directly over me. Incurring additional bruises, I jump down to grab another blanket and pillow, and, having re-ascended (I'm starting to get good at this), arrange myself in a sort of cocoon, with a pillow over my head. Against all odds, I fall asleep almost immediately.

I miss the 0600 watch change, but that's okay, I remind myself, because I was up and around through almost half of the preceding watch. In the galley, deckhand and cook of the day Kim Parks hands me a plate of french toast and bacon wrapped in aluminum foil. Kim, forty-one, is a native of Tangier Island, and he feuds good-naturedly with David Evans, whose family is from Smith Island, Tangier's rival and neighbor, calling him a "Yarney"—a teller of tall tales and an inhabitant of "Yarneytown." David and his family have since moved to Newport News, where he has already purchased a Nissan pickup and looks forward to buying a house. Starting pay with Dann is $115 a day, plus benefits—nothing to sneer at for a high-school dropout just turned eighteen.

"We're on a job that floats," David says. Kim adds, "This coal run means a lot of movement, but as far as Dann Towing goes, it's a great company. We're not here to play, we're here to stay."

Staying means thirty days on board and fifteen days off. There's no such thing as a holiday in the ironclad schedule of Dann's contract with BGE. With a second tug, *New England Coast*, ply-ing the run as well, the coal arrives at the Baltimore generating facilities daily and, aside from the incremental stockpiling of a forty-five-day reserve, is burned almost as fast.

Kim's month-long stint will be finished as of our arrival at Pier Nine, the same as Billy Cahoon's, and he's thrilled at the prospect. He's looking forward to rejoining his wife, Joy, who teaches second grade on Tangier. "I was born and raised on the island, and as far as I'm concerned, that's the only place to be. I'm real homesick."

But then, in defense of his work situation—or possibly be-cause he's talking with someone who's writing down his candid words—Kim adds, "All the time on the move makes your thirty days go by quickly because you're keeping real busy."

Unlike Billy, whose brother will be meeting him at Newport News and driving him home to Belhaven, Kim's son will be in-tercepting us by boat as we pass Tangier Island early tomorrow morning. This sounds like a risky undertaking to me, but to a resident of Tangier, it's nothing if not routine. Kim's replace-ment, a new hire for Dann, will meet us at Pier Nine, as will first mate Billy's, who happens to be *Gulf Coast*'s senior captain, Stanley Barnhart. Stanley is flying in from his home in Tampa, Florida, and I've been forewarned that (1) he is a colorful charac-ter, and (2) his hair hangs down to his waist.

I spend a good part of the morning in the wheelhouse with Jackie Nixon, who fills me in on tug lore as well as his own life. He started working on tugboats at seventeen, when his father passed away. "Tugging has been pretty consistent, pretty good to me," he quietly affirms.

Jackie has seen numerous improvements in equipment and navigation. Back when he first got his master's license, "most tugs were single screw, but few are left." He goes on to explain that the greater horsepower of modern tugs equates with efficiency. Barges are bigger, turnaround times are faster, and, most important, the process of towing is less precarious. There follows some technical talk about *Gulf Coast*: she'll burn about 1500 gallons of diesel fuel down, and 2100 gallons back, or 3600 round trip. She has two 3.5-ton air conditioners, located between the stacks, to compensate for the heat generated by the engine room. No wonder I felt so chilled last night!

Speaking of cold, in the winter of '83 to '84, when Jackie was captain of the Dann tug *Zeus*, he got stuck off Tolchester in a hard freeze with three other tugs and their tows. "The Coast Guard ice-breaker came down to save us. She broke us out, and we just followed her like a bunch of ducks."

He points out that I've seen two out of the three *make-ups*, the term for the tug's relationship to its tow. The first is *alongside*, the second is *tow wire*, and the third is *pushing ahead* or *astern pushing*.

Like the others, he stresses the regularity of the coal run. "We're like a wheel moving, like a ball rolling. Light barge down [the bay], loaded barge up." I ask him which season is better, and he thinks for a minute before he answers, "Summer, because of the safety factor."

But he qualifies this by noting that interference from pleasure boats can be bothersome. Specifically, he singles out sailboaters for their lack of awareness, because so many of them assume they have an inviolable right-of-way, and ever enjoy cutting too closely ahead or astern.

"They don't seem to understand that we don't have brakes."

He goes on to recall a time when, with a tow wire make-up in a narrow channel, he was suddenly bearing down on a sailboat that had jibed into *Gulf Coast*'s path. To warn the sailboat away, Jackie had to resort to the loud-hailer, something he wouldn't normally do.

"There was a lady in a bikini on board, and she stood up and pointed to the sail, real angry-like. She just kept jabbin' her finger at the sail, as if I was some kind of dummy. She was sayin', I guess, that I was supposed to stop dead and let her mosey on by."

If the tug had been in the notch—that is to say, pushing from astern—he might have been able to stop the engines and even reverse the screws (although a full stop would not occur for the better part of a mile). But towing as he was, he had no way of slowing down. A tug captain's second worst nightmare, after that of colliding with another boat, must surely be that of his own barge ramming his stern.

The scent of Kim's roast beef is wafting up the companion-way. There's just enough time before dinner to squeeze in a tour of the engine room with David, who has arrived with more coffee for Jackie. In addition to his other duties, David is in training as interim engineer. He hands me a pair of muff-type hearing protectors, and I follow him below.

Spacious and well lit, with the larger pieces of machinery painted Caterpillar yellow, the engine room has a layout that's easy to grasp. The twin D3512s each have gauge panels indicating, as David marks in the hourly log, that everything's running smoothly. Situated between the main engines are the main and backup generators, as well as the separate engine for the tow winch. Surrounding these are various pumps, air compressors, and air tanks from which compressed air is drawn to crank over the diesels. My eyes follow the exhaust pipes, thickly insulated at the manifolds, as they go up into the stack enclosures. Every length of tubing and conduit is clearly stenciled. In pantomime, David explains what goes where. A mediocre lip-reader, I'm about to lift one muff to hear him better until I realize that the noise is beyond deafening. I can't even hear myself shout.

Retreating through the fiddly to the crew's quarters, I sit down to dinner on the stool beside Billy, who is about to go on watch. With him is deckhand Anthony Foster, also twenty-three, from Heartfield, Virginia, whose father and grandfather both had careers in tugging. On his last day aboard, Kim has prepared an outstanding meal. He's even baked a pan of homemade biscuits. *Con brio*, we take turns carving on the hunk of beef swimming in a stew of potatoes, carrots, and onions. Seconds are followed by thirds, but carve as we might, the roast doesn't seem to get much smaller. The others will be eating right after the watch change: maybe they'll make a dent.

In the afternoon, as the bay slips by, I spend some time in the wheelhouse with Billy. He's explaining to me about non-follow-up steering controls located on the port and starboard sides of the binnacle and on the aft console. A non-follow-up control is like a joystick, as opposed to the main steering lever that acts as an indicator of the rudder. Non-follow-up means that the rudder is moved in a series of taps, each tap a small degree of angle, which is a more precise method of maneuvering than swinging the rudder back and forth like a paddle. Describing all this, Billy's not touching a thing—he's on autopilot.

As we talk, a fast-moving sport fishing boat approaches us at right angles on what appears to be a collision course. Billy watches it with a careful eye but shows no particular concern. The boat cuts right across our bow. Billy just shakes his head.

"They're really pushin' their faith in their equipment," he says. I ask Billy if he has any advice for boaters with respect to commercial traffic on Chesapeake Bay.

"Monitor channel 13," he says, "and realize the limited maneuverability of the big stuff."

He goes on to state that "guesswork involving what the other guy is doing" can lead to potentially dangerous situations. I admire his low-key approach; he's an offshore fisherman himself when on vacation. In one way or another, he contrives to spend the major portion of his life on the water.

We're passing Thimble Light, a red cone-topped cast-iron cylinder rising out of the bay like a tomato can in the middle of nowhere. Training the binoculars on this nineteenth-century classic, I fantasize about what a lighthousekeeper's life must have been like (the light has long since been automated). Anthony arrives in the wheelhouse with a mug of coffee for Billy. Anthony has been working in the forepeak, accessible by hatch from the forward deck, where paint, chain, and mooring line are stored. Over the last few trips between Baltimore and Newport News, the forepeak has been chipped and painted, its bins reorganized. Earlier, he had invited me down for a look, but the paint fumes drove me out. Still, I had seen enough to be impressed by the thoroughness of his handiwork. I take the opportunity now to ask him how he came to tugging.

"First I went into truck driving, but couldn't keep up with my bills," he shrugs. The family tugging tradition was always there as a backup profession. Through an uncle, he got his present job.

"Doing this is a lot better than anything else I've done with my life," he says, and Billy chimes in, "That's exactly how I feel—I was born with salt on my tongue."

Anthony and Billy joke about what Billy's going to do when he gets off the tug. Anthony still has twenty-two days to go, which he crosses out with one diagonal slash per twelve hours on the boxed numerals of the calendar hanging beside the port-hole above the crew's table. Billy, whose vacation starts in an hour or so, has very concrete plans.

"First day back, I'll cut the grass and do yard work, then pay bills, then change the oil in my Corvette."

Nearing Newport News, we pass Old Point Comfort to star-board, and a few minutes later, Fort Wool, where Billy executes a sweeping turn. On both shores at the Hampton Tunnel ap-proaches, automotive traffic, aimed straight toward the water, gradually ramps downward out of sight. Billy starts the winch engine and signals to Anthony on the afterdeck to ease off the drum's brake. The tow wire is reeled in until the barge prow nips at our heels. Off to the port side is Norfolk Naval Base, where thirty years ago I spent twenty-two months on a breakdown-prone fleet oiler that rarely left the pier. The bristling complex-ity of all those gray ships hasn't changed much since then, al-though the aircraft carriers have definitely gotten huger.

We're passing the Navy's mid-channel ammo dock, where ships used to offload munitions before proceeding to shipyard and drydock. I can't tell if the facility is used anymore—quite possibly, weapons technology has rendered it obsolete.

Ahead to starboard lie the coal terminals, Pier Nine (Pier Nine Terminal Company) and its competitor DTA (Dominion Termi-nal Associates), which *Gulf Coast* and *New England Coast* also frequent. The sheer size of these operations boggles the mind—both have separate piers, switchyards, silos, conveyors, stackers, and shiploaders, not to mention coal piles.

We pass over another automotive tunnel, the Monitor-Merrimac, otherwise known as 1-664, and the tugboat *Nancy McAllister* steams over to assist us into Pier Nine. A line is secured from *Nancy* to the stern of the barge. At the same time, the tow wire is reeled in all the way, so that the bridle is directly above our stern (at this point, I could almost reach over and touch the barge prow). Jackie, whose seniority and experience are now required in the wheelhouse, throws the twin screws into reverse. Tension is slacked off the winch, and the shackle at the end of the bridle falls to the deck, where Anthony deftly punches out its pin with a sledgehammer.

Gulf Coast, now free, turns in a quick circle to assist *Nancy* in rotating the barge 180 degrees. With one tug at its bow and one at its stern, *E-4* is brought alongside the pier, each captain coordinating by radio what the other cannot see.

Once the barge lines are secured, both tugs go over to the bulkhead, where they tie up—*Gulf Coast* against the pilings, *Nancy* outboard. Here the tugs wait, away from the worst of the coal dust, while the barge is being loaded. To the accompaniment of a continuous warning siren, the gigantic shiploader and conveyor system rumble to life, and an endless belt of coal rises a hundred feet or so to a horizontally traveling, telescoping chute with a rotating spoon at the bottom of it, which slews and luffs the coal around the interior of *E-4*'s cargo box. With a loading rate of 6500 tons an hour, it'll take seventy minutes to fill the 7800-ton-capacity barge. That's how much liberty I've got on this cruise, just enough time to climb off and look around.

On transferring myself from bulwark to bulkhead, I notice that a taxi has driven up and a man with a very long ponytail is getting out. This must be Captain Stanley Barnhart, just off the plane from Tampa. Also, replacement deckhand Ken Long from Beaufort, North Carolina, is here, a stuffed seabag at his feet. After meeting both newcomers, I excuse myself to walk around.

The sun is setting, the scenery is stupendous. Coal terminals have a weather system all their own: to reduce blowing dust, water is sprayed periodically from conveyor trestles high above the coal piles, forming a mist that refracts in rainbow hues against the leggy equipment. I watch a bulldozer flattening the top of a pile even as it is being added to from above. In one open-ended building, a tandem rotary dumper grips two 100-ton rail-cars at a time and tips them, track and all, until the coal spills out onto a conveyor that grades, sorts, and shunts it to various locations. Pairs of empty railcars roll slowly along the exit spur until they recouple, banging two by two into a deadheaded train.

Without a hard hat, I know that I shouldn't stray far. Looking back to the pier, it's plain to see that E-4's freeboard is shrinking: a peak of coal is visible above the hold combing and the barge doesn't look quite as salient as before. Loaded, E-4's draft will deepen to about fifteen feet; that'll give Gulf Coast the requisite visibility in her wheelhouse to push from behind.

Shortly after I climb back on board, the shiploader shuts down, and directly our lines are cast off. Nancy, preceding us, touches her bow bumper against the barge's prow as Captain Stanley eases our bow into the stern notch. Port and starboard hawsers are looped over the tug's quarter bitts and tightened with the barge's hand-operated wheel winches—a two-person cranking job on each side, repeated several times. When Gulf Coast is snug, the docking captain (the mate from Nancy on the barge with a walkie-talkie) gives departure orders to the tugs. Stanley and his counterpart 350 feet away acknowledge each command with a sharp pull of the whistle lanyard. In tugspeak, the loaded barge is "walked off" from Pier Nine.

Once we're in the channel, Nancy McAllister draws away, hav-ing reclaimed her mate, whose last radio transmission is to wish us a safe trip. Now that we're pushing instead of pulling, there's no longer a frontal feeling of plowing through the water. We've become a rear-end propulsion plant to a long, symmetrical ebony mountain contained within a box. From the wheelhouse, E-4 stretches ahead of us into the gathering night, a negative dimension almost, black within black.

Crossing over the two tunnels now, I watch the headlights disappear below grade and try to imagine the lightless depths beneath West Virginia where this coal originated in seams of compressed organic matter tens of millions of years ago. There's something elemental, almost symbolic, about conveying a load of darkness all the way to Baltimore, where it'll be transmuted into light. The gift we're bearing will meet greater Baltimore's energy needs for slightly more than half a day. *New England Coast*, whose path we'll cross somewhere out on the bay tomorrow, will make up the difference.

The ships of the naval base, dramatically illuminated, recede in the distance. I stand on the afterdeck in the blustery night. Now that the taut and greasy tow wire no longer bisects it, this is a good place to be alone. Beneath my feet, the noise from the engine room is barely contained by the vibrating metal deck. I find the wake mesmerizing; in it, I can distinguish the clockwise and counterclockwise rotation of the screws, propelling in excess of 12,000 not-so-hydrodynamic tons, no unremarkable feat in this ebb tide with the current going against us. My thoughts are cut short when Kim bursts through the fiddly and rushes over.

"We've been looking for you, pal! We thought you'd fallen overboard!" he yells above the ambient din.

"I've been in this spot for the last fifteen minutes," I yell back, "just relaxing and enjoying the night!"

"Well, you gotta let someone know where you are at all times," he reprimands me. "It's mighty dark out there, and you wouldn't stand a chance of being rescued if you fell off and nobody saw you."

I'm somewhat embarrassed to have been the object of concern. Kim obviously has a short-timer's jitters, but I can appreciate what he's saying. A person could flip over the low bulwarks (about thirty inches) of this or any tug—not that anybody would deliberately try to, but it could happen—and the machinery would drown out all cries for help.

I follow him into the deckhouse. The cumulative effects of the day's excitement are beginning to wear on me, and I haven't had supper yet. From an assortment of leftovers and sandwich materials, I fix myself a platter, and not long afterward, I turn in, but I have trouble falling asleep, so many new images are flitting across my mind.

Slumber, when it comes, is fitful. Part of the problem is that I'm unaccustomed to the motion of barge pushing. In the bunk, it's an up-down side-to-side bumping and jolting that is impossible to ignore. A little before 0600, my internal smoke detector awakens me for good when David lights up his first Doral of the day, some three feet directly below my nostrils.

I wanted to get up with the watch change anyway, to see Kim disembark for Tangier. I'm in plenty of time for a helping of hot sausage gravy over toast, but Kim's already gone. At the table, Jackie, just off duty, fills me in on the details: at 0510 hours, two miles south of Smith Point, a small boat, the *Marian Joy*, piloted by Kim's son, drew alongside the barge. Jackie stopped the engines long enough for Kim to climb down in the hazy near-darkness without mishap. I must have been sleeping more soundly than I thought; still, I'd like to have at least waved good-bye.

After breakfast, I ask permission to take a walk on the barge. Stanley, in the wheelhouse, says it's fine with him as long as I wear a work vest and hold on to the safety rail along the hatch combing. "And beware of loose coal," he cautions. "Even with that new nonskid paint on the deck, it can be like stepping on marbles."

As a rule, barges don't have railings around the perimeter. Also, tourists don't go out on barges. Stanley orders David to accompany me in case I do something stupid. We don the work vests, and he crosses over first, vaulting from the tug's quarter bitts to the barge's notch rail, then jumping down—all in the span of a second. Lacking gymnastic prowess, I have difficulty just getting up on the bitts, but I manage by placing a foot on the bulkhead railing of the deckhouse and doing a split. Atop the bitts, I pause, mesmerized by the chafing interface between bow bumper and barge notch—the thing that kept me awake most of the night—until I muster the courage to leap over to the notch rail. From there, without the aid of David's proffered hand, I jump the five feet or so to the deck.

With some trepidation, I follow him along the narrow coal-strewn straightaway between hatch combing and eight-foot drop to moving water. We're walking on the barge's leeward side to cut the wind, but it occurs to me that maybe we should be walking on the windward side, so the stiff breeze would blow me against, instead of away from, the combing if I lost my balance. With each step, I place my feet between coal chunks and reposition my right hand on the safety rail. David, taking no precautions whatsoever, strides blithely to the barge prow before I'm even halfway there.

Eventually, I too get to the prow, where glistening sheets of spray wet the foremost coal. There's no noise up here but the whooshing of water, no vibration. Through the distant reflective windows of the wheelhouse, I can barely make out Stanley drinking coffee and smoking a cigarette. The radar twirls, Old Glory snaps at the signal mast, the diesel exhaust feathers away. All at once, I find myself completely relaxed.

"Hey, it's pretty nice out here, don't you think?"

David agrees, and we stand silently for a minute, imbibing the beauty of the bay apart from the necessities of maintaining commerce and earning a daily wage. Jackie told me earlier that between 1984 and 1992, when he worked in New York harbor, he towed some barges that actually had living quarters on them, but there's no such position as a live–aboard bargeman on the Chesapeake. If there were, I think I might be tempted to apply for the job.

On the way back to the tug, I deliberately step on nuggets of coal and keep my hand off the rail—and feel perfectly safe.

Later in the morning, I attempt to zero in on the essence of tugging during a conversation with Stanley. Looking fit and rested from his recent time off, he projects the charismatic intensity of a person who has had many experiences and isn't afraid to talk about them. In 1965, after dropping out of high school at sixteen, he went to sea with a bunch of his buddies. They enrolled at the Seaman's International Union School in New Orleans.

"We were supposed to be learning the fundamentals of seamanship, but what we really did was slave labor for the union."

After several months of being fed and housed under this arrangement—his buddies soon quit to go back to high school—Stanley received his entry-level Sea Card and got on his first ship, an old Cities Service tanker out of Galveston. His rating was that of a saloon messman—"basically a waiter"—which he hated because he wanted to be up on deck in the fresh air. On this initial voyage, he was denied that opportunity, but when the ship reached its final port, an unexpected thing happened.

"The paymaster just kept putting money in my hand, a whole stack of bills, far more than I thought was due me."

Stanley couldn't believe how much money he had earned.

"I knew I had found my life's work," he says. "From then on, it was just a matter of getting the right kind of duty."

His next ship went to West Africa. He signed on as a deckhand so he could practice the fundamentals of seamanship, and absolutely loved it.

"My friends were back in high school taking math tests, and I was sailing up the Congo River. Man, I felt really sorry for them."

As Stanley talks, I'm looking out at the barge, where a mixed congregation of gulls has alighted. A few sit upon the center peak of coal, but most are in a row on the starboard hatch combing, preening, and staring fixedly into the wind. Occasionally, a white feather is blown across the coal.

"Back then, you had to demonstrate a working knowlege of things like splices. Now, you're lucky if you see a *picture* of a splice."

Stanley goes on to describe how the shipping industry has changed. "Instead of the ro-ros and container ships you see today, there used to be honest-to-goodness freighters with things like wooden hatches and cargo booms."

After a year or two of seafaring, at the height of the Vietnam War, Stanley was about to be drafted into the Army. He figured he was already engaged in the service of his country, because the ships he was on were mainly hauling "bombs and beer" to ports in the South China Sea.

"I was in Da Nang, Quang Tri, Cam Ranh Bay. I was doing my part in the merchant marine."

He tried to get an occupational deferment, but his local draft board turned him down. The union even pleaded his case, but the Selective Service denied the request. Stanley decided to enlist in the Army rather than allow himself to be drafted, with the understanding that he could choose whichever specialty school he wanted.

"I went down the list and picked intelligence encryption because it promised to be as far from the action as possible."

And he was right: he stayed stateside and spent his hitch, after training, in the air-conditioned offices of generals and colonels, repairing their coding equipment.

Upon leaving the Army, Stanley bummed around the country with his first wife. "We camped from Florida to Oregon, taking odd jobs, never staying in one place too long."

Eventually, they settled down on a mountainside in Oregon. It was a harsh, though simple existence; they had to walk to town for supplies because their old car no longer ran and they couldn't afford a new one. They hung in for a number of years, but in the end, with funds nonexistent and his back-to-the-land esprit all but broken, Stanley recommitted himself to his old vocation: ablebodied seamanship. It would doom his marriage and end his dream for privacy and space, but he felt he had no choice. He was lucky to have his non-expired union card.

"The definition of luck is when preparation meets opportunity," he interjects sagely. "It was time to move on."

Ill at ease with the modernization of the shipping industry, he switched to tugging and stayed. "I liked the smaller scale, the fact that a deckhand could still be a deckhand and not a goddamn specialist."

Earning his mate's and master's licenses, he steadily expanded his responsibilities. As tug captain, he made his share of professional mistakes, but each one led to greater technical skill and confidence. He learned that marine towing companies were reluctant to hire inexperienced captains. "They'd tell you, if you haven't done damage, they didn't want you."

As captain of *Gulf Coast* since 1988, Stanley is undoubtedly responsible for some of her cosmetic dings and scratches, but when he's in the wheelhouse, he's as meticulous and methodical as anyone could imagine a captain to be.

"I've still got all my fingers and toes," he says. "On this kind of job, that's saying a lot."

I ask Stanley about the burden of command—does it ever wear him down? He looks over at me and chuckles. "No, not really. Basically, I follow two rules: first, keep the boat afloat; second, stay on the boat."

"I'm down in Tampa, kicking back for fifteen days, doing what normal guys do at home, and then I return to this." With a wave of his hand, he indicates the scope of his responsibility— which, as I think about it, includes not only the tug and barge and the lives of those aboard, but also the well-being of several million electricity consumers.

"But I wouldn't want it any other way. As I said, this is my life's work. I realized it back when I was seventeen, when all that money was thrust in my hand."

At forty-seven, Stanley has no plans to retire. He likes leading two separate lives in two distinct parts of the country. He sees his vocation as part of a yin-yang cycle. "After thirty days, you're tired of the boat and the boat is tired of you."

Reverberating with the homilies of this pony-tailed, chain-smoking tug and zen master, I take my leave. I need some fresh air, and I think Stanley needs a break from all my questions. Outside, I stand at the railing just below the wheelhouse windows and breathe deeply for a few minutes, until I realize that what I'm inhaling doesn't quite have the unadulterated salt tang of the bay. Stupid me: I'm breathing coal dust blowing off the barge! It's insidious stuff, infiltrating everything. Earlier, Stanley had told me how he'd changed batteries in the hand-held calculator on the chart desk and noticed an accumulation of coal dust in the tiny sealed compartment. Perhaps the carbon particulate is to blame for the broken radar repeater.

My nose detects the aroma of dinner for the upcoming watch, so I head below. David, cook of the day, has prepared a sizeable feast. On the table sits a roast chicken that looks more like a small turkey, and serving dishes of three vegetables *plus* a huge pot of mashed potatoes, another pot of stuffing, and a pitcher of gravy. On top of this, he's baked a couple of dozen dinner rolls. It's a four-star, four-square meal, and, as usual, there's enough for everybody to indulge in seconds and thirds. All I can say is, for a guy just turned eighteen, his mother sure taught him how to be indispensable.

The meal puts me in a ruminative and lazy mood for the remainder of the afternoon. It'll seem strange, going back to that other reality, the one of tug-watching instead of tug-riding. On the other hand, I'm glad to have been less than three days away from home, and not thirty. We slide under the Bay Bridge and set our course along the familiar deepwater channels.

Just after the 1800 watch change, with Stanley back at the helm, *Gulf Coast* has slowed to quarter speed on the final waterway leading to BGE's unloading pier. The pier, which I hadn't been able to see clearly two nights ago, is long and skeletal, with twelve evenly spaced concrete dolphins—enough room to accommodate at least three coal barges end-to-end. In the center of the pier stands the unloader, a digging contraption of wide rotary scoops that is lowered into a barge as it is shoved backward and forward.

Once *E-4* is secured at the pier, *Gulf Coast* will release from the notch and go over to the bulkhead to drop me off. After that, she'll return to help move the barges along the dolphins, and then, within two hours—after a short break for refueling and grocery shopping—she'll be picking up the next available empty barge.

chapter
12

To live beside Chesapeake Bay is to invest in an intangible. On the face of it, this seems like a misleading assertion, given the very tangible investment that goes into the acquisition of a bay-front home. There's nothing intangible about property taxes or insurance premiums either, or the cost of upkeep as a result of often severe weather, not to mention the high heating bills in winter. The payoff to all these outlays would seem tangible, too: the ever-absorbing waterview, the birdwatching, the boating, the sunsets.

But the real profit comes after the novelty wears off, when the sum of the expenditure has led to a new pattern of living—when the rhythm of the tide is a given, and the restful distancing of one's eyes toward the far horizon is taken for granted. Then, the bayshore dweller is led to a deeper intuitive grasp, to the concept of the *edge*, and what it means to endure in a location that is figuratively next door to everything.

Here I must insert a paragraphic rejoinder: the experience of which I speak is not to be confused with the oft-bandied phrase, *living on the edge*, with its overtones of pop daredevildom and riskiness; nor should it be associated with a kind of sharpness, such as a knife or razor edge, also metaphorically exploited by the symbol surfers of commerce. As I refer to it, the experience has nothing to do with competition either: I hardly think of myself as having an *edge* on anybody, now or in the past. Nor is the experience—to the disappointment, perhaps, of those seeking a psychological definition—used to indicate the reputed fine line between sanity and insanity.

The edge-dwelling I'm talking about, here in the place where land stops and water continues, signifies an ending and a beginning. Not only has it marked an omega and an alpha of marital time frames for K and me, it has also defined itself as a borderline between two lives, the one left behind and the one started anew. For us, this edge represents a stepping-off (or jumping-off) point to the future—a point of no return. Having made our commitment here, we like to imagine it'll lead to a host of upbeat eventualities. (Both of us will be very disappointed if it only brings more of the same old thing.) This edge presages change for us, no matter how inconspicuously it unfolds. People in our shoes know that an edge can be teetered on, but not forever.

Until moving here, I never gave much thought to any of this. I had had no edge experience save brief vacations at seaside once in a while, and on these occasions I was so caught up in the novelty of spending a little time in a bona fide resort, much like the thrill-seekers arriving in Tolchester Park, that I hardly bothered to analyze the wider ramifications. I was escaping, pure and simple. My normal circumstance meant being ensconced in the center of somewhere—a city, a suburb, a rural community—that I would flee temporarily, but in no time at all I'd be packing up and heading back to the center, back to the security and familiarity of the middle. There I was likely to stay because it augured such a predictable existence, such a sure bet. Even during those periods when life wasn't that predictable and all bets were off, it never occurred to me to stray too far afield, so ingrained was my self-restricting sense of place.

Arriving, with K, at this edge took resoluteness; ours was a joint decision to press forward without flinching. Looking back at the way we cobbled the deal together, on little more than a shoestring, verges on the cocksure, a credit to the chutzpah of our slightly younger selves. Yet here we are, rounding the seasons of our second year, with all the cabinets and closets full, feeling rather settled in. Goldenrod and wild asters herald another fall. Fruit is ripening on the persimmon tree. The onion grass, mown for one last time, adds piquancy to the musty scent of the woods

across the road. As nights grow cool, crickets and daddy longlegs
re-invade the kitchen, dying wasps half-heartedly explore win-
dowpanes, fat lost flies circle aimlessly. Spiders have long set up
shop in undusted corners. We even have a newspaper delivered
now—an indicator, if there ever was one, that our roots are becoming established. Outside on the lawn, dogwoods are beginning to blaze purple, while hollies, their berries reddening, are
waxing their most verdant and sassafras are shedding curls of
ochre. One thing I don't have to do around here is rake leaves,
because the wind does it for me; still, it won't be long before I'm
climbing the ladder to unburden the roof gutters.

The warm weekdays draw more pleasure boaters than normal—final flings before haul-outs. Twice I've spotted the sailboat
that once belonged to my former father-in-law, last seen (both
boat and skipper) some twenty years ago. Another ghost from
the past is a cruise liner on which I was once a passenger; it
glides by in the night like a diamond-encrusted oasis, a mega
flame for moths. Among the usual sampling of ships are some
new sightings: a cable layer, a three-masted training vessel from
Sweden, a World War II–era Victory freighter, an oceanographic
something-or-other. As a result of my recent voyage, I avidly
scrutinize every tugboat.

The Coast Guard cutter *Spencer* (*WMEC-905*), with its forward three-inch gun turret and aft helicopter hangar, steams
by, and then the equally albino *Peter W. Anderson*, envoy of the
Environmental Protection Agency. One morning there's a fake
Mississippi riverboat, its paddle-wheel not quite in synch with
its progress. Another morning, I spot the *Pride of Baltimore II*,
the rakish two-masted reproduction of a reproduction that sank,
with loss of life, in an Atlantic storm some ten years ago. For
several Mondays and Tuesdays in a row, a treat of the first order
glides into view: three oyster skipjacks (*Thomas Clyde, Rebecca
T. Ruark,* and *H.R. Krentz*) dredging right offshore, propelled by
their stubby pushboats—sail-less, but nevertheless as picturesque a throwback as anyone could wish for.

For recreation on weekends, we take up the unfinished chores of gardening. K carts home end-of-season specials on mums and orphaned perennials from the local landscape center, and I, as chief spade wielder, am called on to help put them in. Sometimes, thanks to our diligence, it's hard to know where to plant; in supposedly bare patches, I wince when I find myself slicing through buried bulbs. Geraniums and dracaenas need to be potted and moved indoors, and when that's finished, a variety of late-bloomers need watering. The peonies cry out for relocation; where they're growing now, the wind seems to traumatize them. We're also expanding our daffodil, jonquil, and narcissus beds, in anticipation of that many-months-away delirium when cheery things will start popping out of the ground again. In one Sunday's joint effort, we install over two hundred spring bulbs—a property-wide project and a model of spousal teamwork, too, although my wife catches a bad case of poison ivy and, later, we note with dismay that a squirrel has been hard at our heels, digging up select examples of our handiwork.

I have accustomed myself to getting a good night's sleep despite the ambient shuffle of the surf and the reverberation of marine propulsion, despite the moaning of the propane furnaces at either end of the house, despite the inter-joist skittering of a mouse. My dreams are no longer interrupted by sudden scratchings of wind, cracking branches, herons' cackling. But rubbing my eyes after a night's rest and drawing open the curtains, I still can't quite believe the vast ethereal expanse beyond the brushy bank. The sun, peeking through the woods along the driveway, tints the bay like a proscenium bathed by pink footlights, and I am front row in the darkened theater, waking to an extravaganza I could kick myself for sleeping through. Hurriedly, I dress and go out to feed the cats and fetch the newspaper. Morning unfolds like grand opera, vignette upon vignette—breezes chorusing, vessels soloing, clouds scheming, whitecaps tittering, shorebirds cajoling. Such superlative entertainment reduces breakfast to a series of program notes. The newspaper sometimes goes unread.

I have come to take for granted the atmospheric clarity that prevails here despite the sulphuric billowings ten miles across the water. If I decide, at some stopping point during the day, to go down the steps, scramble over the rip-rap and take a stroll along the beach, I can do so without being appalled by what has washed up (among the recent jetsam: half-decomposed rockfish heads with blue plastic I.D. bands—from a Maryland Department of Natural Resources study—fastened through their gills). The spry bay surf, its pebbly shushing, and the sudden drawdown, then flood, from the draft displacement of a passing ship, are familiar to me now. A connoisseur am I of crabpot markers, those styrofoam bobbers skewered by a length of plastic pipe, both severed ashore and pot-tied a couple of hundred feet out.

I accept the bad weather when it comes, look forward to it almost, for I realize that I have consciously chosen, in dwelling on a coastal overlook, to live in harm's way. Gray, the water is as spectacular as it is blue, and so is the sky, its marbled mirror in mood. When the wind whips into a gale and the rain pelts horizontally and tide runs high, damage can be in the offing, and I accept that, too. Pounded incessantly, the base of the unprotected bluff is often scoured out, and then the saturated, deeply riveted slope directly above it collapses. If new sand isn't brought in simultaneously by wave action, the net result is a loss—and a loss of real estate value as well.

Our edge is also prey to a more insidious inclemency: water pollution caused by nutrient overloading. The recent outbreaks of a toxic form of *Pfiesteria piscicida*—a common dinoflagellate, one of hundreds of normally benign microbes found in the bay and its tributaries—have occurred too close for comfort. The injurious dinoflagellate leaves a telltale signature on its fish victims in the form of suppurating coin-sized lesions, and in humans, exposure can result in a variety of ailments: diarrhea, stomach cramps, headaches, short-term memory loss, respiratory and bronchial infections, and colds that escalate to pneumonia.

In shore areas where farming, industry, and housing development have eliminated forests, wetlands, and other wild habitats, phosphorus- and nitrogen-rich runoff flows quickly into the water, creating microbe hyper-breeding grounds. On the Pokomoke River, which drains from the lower peninsula, the haywire *Pfiesteria* is blamed for killing hundreds of thousands of fish and sickening dozens of people.

During the past year, sections of the Pokomoke and other bay tributaries have been temporarily closed to fishing and recreation in an effort to minimize the microbe's impact. Although the danger apparently subsides with the onset of cooler weather, word of mouth and media attention have propelled the *Pfiesteria* scare into a near panic. As a result, the public has lost confidence in the wholesomeness of Chesapeake Bay seafood, and watermen's and seafood suppliers' livelihoods are put in jeopardy. Who's to blame? Finger-pointing leads to heated bickering among state officials and politicians. To re-instill trust, the governor of Maryland is videotaped in his shirtsleeves, munching crabcakes and slurping oyster stew, but he comes across as a bit of a dunderhead—where is his ounce of prevention?

Among the proven perpetrators of the *Pfiesteria* outbreaks are poultry growers, who, entrenched throughout the Delmarva peninsula, are economic players not to be trifled with. Poultry-raising facilities, those malodorous warehouses in which tens of thousands of birds lead short lives of maximum weight gain, generate inordinate amounts of manure, and although this nutrient-rich end product is mostly used as fertilizer,[1] there's too much of it to spread around. Consequently, it gets overapplied, saturating the runoff and contributing to massive blooms of algae that overwhelm the ecosystem. Bay floor grasses, choked of oxygen, die in the polluted water, which becomes a haven for greater numbers of bacteria and other microorganisms, resulting in the estuary's food chain falling out of balance.

Although scientists have no trouble identifying the underlying mechanism of a *Pfiesteria* outbreak, there's a general lack of consensus on what to do about it. In any scenario, the reduction and containment of over-enriching nutrients is a two-edged sword: curtail the source of the problem, and economic viability is held back as well. The poultry growers scream to high heaven that the degradation of the bay environment isn't their fault alone, and they're right. All chemically dependent farming methods boost the nutrient load. Leaving fields fallow over wintertime instead of planting cover crops, for example, not only causes richer runoff but makes more of it. Add to this the outflow from industries too legion to enumerate, and it's obvious that the bay's good health is assaulted from all sides. If you want to get nitpicky, just about every citizen of the five-state watershed is culpable as well—anybody who drives a car, flushes a toilet, waters a lawn, or, wittingly or unwittingly, uses some form of herbicide, fungicide, or pesticide to improve their quality of life.

The bay and its tributaries can be pictured as the collection basin for a broad swath of interactivity, from agriculture-dense rural to business-intense urban, connected by an infrastructure of streets and highways, whose runoff alone contains almost every hydrocarbon particle and poisonous molecule known to humankind. The scene in its entirety looks something like this: a gurgling network of drains including P-traps, S-traps, waste pipes, roof gutters, downspouts, curb grates, storm sewers, road-side culverts, septic tanks, settling tanks, treatment plants—all of which join, at one juncture or another, the gullies, creeks, marshes, and rivers. This monumental flushing system ends up in the open water here, where many pollutants settle or remain in suspension, due to the Chesapeake's breadth, shallowness, and limited tidal action.

In the mid-Atlantic region, estuarine life has reached a point where it can barely hold its own against society's onslaught. The citizenry personifies the opposite of stasis; its watchwords are *bigger, better, faster, sexier*. It won't settle for anything less than *new and improved*. Imagineers dream up consumer ticklers, market analysts ferret out coming trends, manufacturers tool up product lines to nullify everything cranked out previously. The perception of economic vigor is a given, and water inevitably fits into the schemes of hype and profit, for it is water that redeems the sins of daily excess. Water bears away every woe, every logjam; it is the ticket to forgetfulness, to letting go of old technology and moving ahead with the new. As the rain laves parking lots, it also launders dirty air. Water cools energy-producing facilities (and powers a precious few in its own right) and allows for the necessary discharge from factories. And upon water is built the edifice of modern sanitation, that sublime guarantor of human dignity actualized with the twist of a handle.

As receptor of all that flows into it, Chesapeake Bay is at the cutting edge of a new identity. Instead of the inexhaustible harvest ground of yore, it is in danger of becoming a fished-out, crabbed-out, oystered-out dead sea that may never regain its former fecundity. Instead of offering unlimited recreational opportunities for boaters and swimmers, it might turn into just another polluted waterway with posted advisories on where not to swim, where not to fish. Instead of fostering a culture unique to its eastern and western shores, the bay could be so assaulted, then assimilated by mainstream commercialization, that there'd be little left—aside from the grudging panorama of the nitrous oxide twilight—to commend its beauty.

The pleasure seekers will keep arriving, however, for all the old reasons. Watercraft will undoubtedly multiply, creating weekend gridlock far worse than what we witness today, but the people aboard may be donning protective gear in addition to life vests, lest they inadvertently be exposed to some sickening ether. The shipping channels will be busier than ever, so busy that mishaps might be nigh unavoidable. If cargo spills become routine, lawmakers could be led to relax environmental standards in order to convince the public that everything's hunky-dory. *What's a little oil slick?—hell, there ain't nothin' livin' in there anyhow!* The nostalgia market will thrive by leaps and bounds, for old days and old ways will be fondly remembered in logo and insignia, and there'll even be an ancient skipjack or two plying for charter, available (at a stiff fee) for weddings, banquets, family reunions, funerals. The once-colorful watermen, too, will be feted, and their tongs, crab pots, and seines touted as objets d'art, appreciated for their economy of design rather than their

usefulness, which will be described only in coffeetable books nobody bothers to read. The bed & breakfasts will be hermetically
sealed, the maritime museums will have downloaded into CD-
ROMs, the beaches will have sensors embedded in the sand to
warn off picnickers . . . oh, it is a future I'm quite sure I don't
want any part of!

The bay is at the edge because civilization itself is at the edge.
What transpires in the twenty-first century will likely deter-
mine the fate of centuries to come. Will humankind pile up in-
surmountable problems, then cave in to less democratic forms of
government that will perfect the art of concealing the sad bad
news of slow but sure extinction? Will we, befoulers nonpareil of
our own planet, shoot for the stars in a last-ditch effort to rid
ourselves of the mess we've made? Will we be deceived by socio-
political claptrap that insists on looking at the bright side, to the
detriment of the unvarnished truth? Already, public opinion is
manipulated at the drop of a pin. Where there's spin, there's in-
fluence, but the pitch is so damnably subtle that we don't know
it's hitting us even as we ante up for the product. What we discriminating world-viewers turn down or turn away from, our
progeny embrace with a vengeance—ye olde pendulum swing. Is
it just possible that the whole game's going to fold? Will cliques
of nomads roam where mighty cities stood? Will the rise and fall
occur in so short a span that grandparents will have time, but
grandchildren won't?

The edge I stand on can be construed as an abyss, not that I
relish perceiving it as such, but I do feel the necessity for hedging
my bets. These final moments of the twentieth century hold so
much promise that it hurts. Humankind's worst scourges are on
the verge of extinction, dictators are in jail or at least in the dog-
house, intercontinental friendships are blossoming on the Inter-
net, technology is empowering truly creative thinking (as opposed to war ruminations), and people in greater numbers than
ever before are enjoying the benefits of an improved standard of
living. Yet the void stretches before us—the running out of fossil
fuels, the nuclear Pandora's box that is looking more and more

like an accident waiting for a place to happen, the apathy toward political processes, the terrible swift sword of terrorism, the consequences of overpopulation, the dumbing down of education, the crumbling inner cities, and, now more than ever, the immemorial bugaboo of the rich getting richer and the poor getting poorer. To subscribe to a palmy, if not rosy, outlook in spite of the mounting evidence is to hide our heads in the sand. There's trouble ahead, make no mistake about it—but hasn't human progress ever been thus?

Before Chesapeake Bay is relegated to a posterity such as I describe, with slender hope of its ever being rehabilitated to an approximation of its bounteous past, we need to act. The worst hasn't happened yet, even though there's every indication that the curve of degradation could approach the flat line. A visitor as far back as Captain John Smith recognized the bay's abundant variety of life and set great store by it. Three centuries later, while that variety can no longer be characterized as abundant, with few exceptions it is still extant, awaiting an environmentally gentler hand. We need to appeal to our better selves and conquer our all-too-human tendencies toward greed and indifference. If, for instance, we can preserve and even enlarge what's left of the bay's buffer strips and wetlands, we can restore habitats for spawning fish such as shad and menhaden, as well as for ducks, geese, eagles, turkey, and migratory songbirds. Studies show that forest buffers alone can remove 90 percent of runoff-borne nitrogen and phosphorous—pollution that is directly implicated in the runaway toxicity of normally harmless *Pfiesteria*.

Given the slowness and unpredictability of any hypothetical turnaround to good health, the bay may be likened to a patient in remission for the foreseeable future. Restrictions severely limiting hunting and fishing are likely to remain in place for generations. The enormous crab and oyster harvests of yore will probably never be repeated. Efforts to educate the populace throughout the length and breadth of a watershed covering nearly 150,000 square miles will have to be backed up by stringently enforced anti-pollution laws on the local level. From upstate

New York to southern Virginia, awareness of Chesapeake Bay can no longer be an option of passing interest for the few, but a penally reinforced code of conduct for the many. On the bay itself, boaters and watermen need to self-police their activities with a greater sense of responsibility. At water's edge, dwellers like K and me must be vigilant about what we do *for* rather than *against* the intrinsic order of things. Curtailing senseless self-aggrandizement starts at home. A bay view like ours is a lucky privilege, not a mortgage-guaranteed right.

The bay can be saved if its presence can somehow be woven into the great national hierarchy of values. Distant cities and rural communities that have no ties to the Chesapeake other than the unseen sloping bond of gravity need to register a more sensitive, more knowledgeable affinity. Of the tens of millions of people whose jobs and lifestyles have an impact on the bay, few, I would imagine, would knowingly want to put it at further risk. The phrase "Save the Bay" needs to jump off posters and license plates and into hearts and minds. If the estuary can be elevated to the status of a treasured cultural icon right now—not as a reaction to a deteriorated future—it will be assured survival and something more: a renewed capacity to flourish.

So the edge is not just a perception of where I am, overlooking the water, but the very water itself, the medium that will be ebbing and flowing, same as always, long after my edge has crumbled into alluvium. From this stakeout on Mitchell's Bluff, I want to believe that we *will* live in a better world, a place where all estuarine waters will be pure, a place where the responsibilities for this or any watershed will be met. It doesn't have to be an ideal world, but it does need to be a practical one, in which the threat of human-caused environmental calamity will have become passé simply because humanity's survival will be given a much higher priority than it currently enjoys. The complexity of interrelated natural resources must be fully understood by the many. Active monitoring by the experts must never stop. Only then, perhaps, can legislative courage in combination with executive fiat head off—not stave off—the fate nobody wants.

To get from here to there, we have to address our most pressing concerns one by one, namely pollution in every subtle and obvious manifestation, and continue to insist on controls that will undo our shortsighted habits. We must plan for the long haul—things have gotten pretty far out of hand. Energy-wise alone, the status quo may have to continue for decades because there's so much capital investment to be depreciated, but eventually the tall stacks will need to be staunched and the reactors and refineries shut down. Contemporaneously, alternative sources of power will be brought on line, but with them, our addiction to willy-nilly consumerism will have to end.

Technology will rise to fill the gap, I have no doubt, but from my bewildering millennial vantage, with so many options to choose from, I don't pretend to know what or which it will be, or how it will be implemented. Will we eventually eschew the multi-laned ribbons of pavement that weave around and through the corporate-complected landscape? Will we turn into a race of screen-watching chair-sitting virtual realists? The future predictors have fooled themselves before and will fool themselves again. Cars and computers are central to our existence right now, but who's to say their importance won't be diminished, or even negated, as the decades go by? The changes we're *not* banking on will most likely be the very ones to hit us between the eyes. It is always safe to say that behavioral modifications are coming, if not in the short term, then in the time it takes the whole concrete-and-fiberoptic edifice to superannuate and wear out. For wear out it will, and when it does, we can only trust that the underpinnings of Nature haven't worn out as well, lest our posterity be truly lost, and our noblest inventions squandered.

The car is in the garage, the computer is turned off. My wife and I are standing side by side at the edge of the bluff, looking out over the water. The late afternoon light is lovely this time of year when the bay calm, framed by turning leaves, is an outspread cobalt counterpane beneath the gathering sunset. Within our separate craniums, thoughts are churning, ordinary thoughts that arise from every stimulation both in the distance and at hand, and of these, we share the most interesting ones. We are two pairs of eyes and ears distilling to one, and we are cognizantly sharper for our collaboration. We laugh about how we can never grow tired of what we have because there is so much of it.

We discuss the recent good news: Tolchester is saved from the dredging spoils. After the muscle flexing of the grass-roots legal counteroffensive, the proposal has been grudgingly withdrawn—nobody knows quite why, although it appears that two local families have formed a corporation to purchase one of the farms.

As K and I watch, the gloaming descends, revealing a faint broken necklace of incandescence along the Western Shore. Far and near, channel buoys have begun winking red and green. To our left, down on the beach, a heron stands sentry-like just inside the wave reach. A pair of cormorants buzz the water, alighting clownishly on tilted pound net posts. A tug with a barge chugs by. High overhead, vees of geese honk their way back to the gabble-gobble ground of the cornfields. The dark house sits behind us, where the cats await feeding and supper awaits fixing, where windows will need to be closed and storm sashes lowered before the advent of cold weather, the harbinger of which caresses us now that sundown's aftermath is fading south of the Baltimore skyline. Below us, the slop and slosh against the riprap goes on and on and on. We stand and imbibe the eternal moment for as long as we can, and then we go indoors.

Notes

NOTES TO CHAPTER ONE

1. A victory for the local militia. Among those killed was the leader of a British landing party, Captain Sir Peter Parker, age twenty-eight, whose mortal remains were returned to England for burial.

2. In the 1920s, the surveyor was paid in lots, in lieu of money, for his work.

NOTES TO CHAPTER SIX

1. These were to be fifty-five 40′ × 100′ lots around the perimeter of the park itself. Also planned were about a hundred 80′ × 100′ commercial and/or residential lots, between the bayfront and the first parallel avenue, as well as other odd-sized lots that fit the subdivision's topographic extremities.

2. Vociferously opposing and ultimately defeating the proposal were (1) the Tug Boat Captain's Association, which considered such a lengthy structure a hazard to navigation, and (2) the Pennsylvania Railroad, operators of the Delmarva-serving N.Y.P.&N. [New York, Philadelphia, and Norfolk] line, which feared the route would be used by truckers to haul Eastern Shore produce to Baltimore, thus depriving the railroad of existing freight revenues.

3. The lots are situated significantly beyond the proposed boardwalk area.

4. In her pamphlet, "A History of Tolchester," May 1982, distributed by the Ladies' Auxilliary of Tolchester.

NOTES TO CHAPTER NINE

1. This was the same parcel, more or less, purchased by John M. Mendinhall and Harry M. Pierce fifty years later.

2. Kent County land records: Land patent, William Toulson, 520 acres, liber 15, folio 205; liber 19, folio 286; 1676.

3. Mitchell House still stands and is currently a bed & breakfast.

4. An extract from the purchase and sale agreement. A more complete account of these early years can be found in David C. Holly's excellent *Steamboat on the Chesapeake: Emma Giles and the Tolchester Line* (Tidewater Publishers, Centreville, MD, 1987).

5. Other accounts state that William was only blind and his wife, Lenore, was deaf—and neither of them was dumb.

6. Perhaps the only surviving structure from Tolchester Park, the bandstand was moved to St. Michaels, where it currently stands on the grounds of the Maritime Museum.

7. The Ferris wheel, for some reason, remains undocumented in photographs. It may not have stood for very long.

NOTES TO CHAPTER TWELVE

1. More recently (and quietly) it is also used as cattle feed.